Praise for *Imp...*

"As a business owner it's all too easy to wake up one day and find that your business and indeed your life – feel out of control. Impact Your Business gives you the inspiration – and the nuts and bolts advice – you need to deal with the challenges and be the success you KNOW you can be."

- Anita Campbell, CEO, SmallBizTrends.com

"My peer entrepreneurs and I tire of those who overcomplicate our financial bookkeeping and accounting. Ken Kaufman does just the opposite. By demystifying financial reporting, without wavering on its utmost importance, he delivers a true gem to business owners."

- Randy Shumway, CEO, The Cicero Group

"An enjoyable read that weaves financial learning into a story, making concepts easy to understand."

- Barbara Weltman, President, Big Ideas for Small Business, Inc.;
Small business advocate, www.barbaraweltman.com.

"*Impact Your Business* will smack every entrepreneur right between their financial and emotional eyes. Whether you're in your first year of business or your twentieth, *Impact Your Business* will stop you in your tracks and open your mind to amazing insights and strategic ideas for the future of your business, and quite possibly your family life. Ken Kaufman does a masterful job with his allegory in connecting the seemingly mind numbing details of business finance into an intriguing adventure with proven steps to success!"

- Tom Metcalf, entrepreneur and President, Telenotes Inc.

"Ken shares specific, pragmatic solutions to problems that plague most entrepreneurs-- definitely worth reading!"

- Ben Peterson, successful entrepreneur and angel investor;
Co-Founder & CEO, BambooHR

"Wow! This story is what all entrepreneurs have experienced. I see a lot of myself in it, and I can relate. Masterfully told in fiction, all the trials and tribulations of being a small business owner are given life, and then solved. In *Impact Your Business*, Ken Kaufman really delivers a must read for everyone that owns a business or is seeking to start a business!"

- Lee Mullis, President & CEO, L&R Integrity

"As the CFO of multiple small businesses one of my largest challenges is helping entrepreneurs truly understand and properly manage cash flow and profitability. *Impact Your Business* is a phenomenal new tool that helps teach these principles in a clear, unintimidating way."

- Steve Guymon, President, Simple CFO

"Earlier in my career as a first-time CEO of a struggling business, I can attest first-hand to some of the same challenges Steve Loveland faces in *Impact Your Business*. I can only imagine how different my outcome would have been had I followed the IMPACT model. IMPACT will definitely be the financial foundation for all future ventures--I only wish I had found it sooner in my career."

- Dan Fellars, Founder, Subscriptive in Nature

"As a business owner and management consultant for dozens of small/midsized companies over the past 20 years, I have a keen awareness that "cash is king" when it comes to business survival and longevity. *Impact Your Business* is very unique in that it reveals a raft of hard hitting concepts in a crisp, entertaining way. Although the ideas are profound, they are presented in a manner that is crystal clear and immediately useable by entrepreneurs of any background."

- John Boyd, President, J Curve Sales;
Author of *The Illustrated Guide to Selling You*

"Imagine listening to a presenter tell you to 'move from qualitative data to quantitative data in order to improve performance, decision-making, acumen, and success.' Boring, right? Not so in *Impact Your Business*. Ken has woven an interesting allegorical account that not only draws you into the story, but crystallizes, simply, the importance of understanding, interpreting, and applying the numbers. I thought I'd read a few pages and put the book aside--I didn't. I couldn't. I read the entire thing, and highly recommend it to every entrepreneur and entrepreneur wanna-be who intends to be successful in their venture."

- Cindy Kraft, the CFO-Coach

"I look forward to Ken Kaufman's e-newsletters. He's an original thinker who always provides at least one nugget of useful information I've never heard before. Now he's taken that same insight and turned it into a readable, relatable book that entrepreneurial business owners are sure to devour in one sitting. Written in an entertaining, highly-accessible style, the allegory format makes it easy to understand the financial challenges we all face, as well as the real-world solutions we all need. *Impact Your Business* comes at just the right time, giving us clarity, empowerment and even hope."

- Brian Rouff, Managing Partner, Imagine Marketing

"*Impact Your Business* is a must-read for any small business leader. I am giving a copy of this book to everyone on my team and the executive team including the CEO, COO, and CMO. There is no other book like this on the market. Basic finance and accounting topics are presented in a comprehensive and accessible format. The fictional story makes the book a quick read and a page-turner. Applying the principles set out in this book will *Impact Your Business* in a very positive way."

- Mike Campbell, CPA, CFO

"The best consultants are great teachers, and Ken Kaufman proves that he is the real deal with this wonderful book. Much like the financial management approach that Ken recommends,

Impact Your Business meets the IMPACT criteria--insightful, meaningful, precise, accessible, comparative and timely. Thanks, Ken, for reminding me why I got into this business--to help others accomplish their dreams. I can't wait to share your work with my own clients."

- JoAnne M. Berg, CPA;
Founder and CEO, PEER Coaching Network, Inc.

"By highlighting 'best practices' in an entertaining allegory, the author has provided practical and priceless insights into helping entrepreneurs succeed in business."

- Roger Andrus, Executive Director, Provo Tech Xelerator

"Ken Kaufman has done what I scarcely thought possible - presenting principles of sound financial management in a way that is accessible and even **fun** to read. By reading this book, entrepreneurs who normally find such topics hard to swallow will gain the skills and clarity they need to succeed. The narrative format is so engaging that I found myself building skills I'd long avoided, but desperately needed."

- Dr. Daniel Crosby, President, Crosby Performance Consulting

"Ken Kaufman just gets it. He understands people and he understands the bottom-line. More importantly, he understands the impact people have on the bottom-line. Take the time to read *Impact Your Business*. It won't just impact your business - it will impact your life."

- D.J. Allen, co-author of *The Xs & Os of Success:*
A Playbook for Leaders in Business and Life

"As an entrepreneur and business owner, I couldn't help but be very impressed with Ken Kaufman's new book, *Impact Your Business*. I thought it might be like a lot of other business books that I have read, but I was very pleasantly surprised and immediately drawn into the allegory. Not only is it well written in a style that is easy to understand and relate to, it also covers the challenges that every entrepreneur struggles with in the growth of a business. It also clearly explains the benefits of including a part-time CFO as part of the management team of a growing company. As the co-founder and CEO of a company that provides part-time general counsel attorneys to growing companies, I whole-heartedly support this premise!"

- Stuart Blake, CEO, The General Counsel, LLC

"Whether you are contemplating a new business, just starting out, or a seasoned business owner, you will find this book has simple yet sound advice to help keep you on course in the perilous business climate of our times."

- Brian Long, President, SpectraSeven Inc.

"*Impact Your Business* continues to amplify the success of our company. Any entrepreneur can relate to the story of Steve and his journey through business ownership. Understanding the IMPACT concept gave me peace with the financial uncertainty of being an entrepreneur by getting to the roots of managing finances. This book provides the roadmap for the goal of achievement and is a MUST for business owners and financial leaders in your organization."

- Crystina Scott, President, ASL Communication

"Having been an accounting and tax professional for over 25 years and then adding business intermediary skills, I found *Impact Your Business* to be absolutely on point. The allegory is one I see on almost a daily basis. The book gives clear, easy to understand direction to issues that most business owners are afraid to address because of the perceived complexity. Impact *Your Business* gives and easy and entertaining way to understand the most critical issues that face all business owners. If you own or want to own a successful business, this is a must read!"

- Janet Ackerson, EA, CBI;
CFO, Dimension Business Brokers

"Ken has me working brain muscles I didn't even know I had. Fresh perspective breeds fresh ideas, and *Impact Your Business* does a better job than any at shedding a new light on business decisions. It's as simple as it is useful!"

- Anthony Castro, President, Exceptional Accounting Services, LLC

"*Impact Your Business* provides refreshing and imperative insights for business leaders to gain (and maintain) a solid competitive advantage using the often overlooked functions of accounting and finance. Told from the engaging and captivating perspective of the fictional character, Steve Loveland, Mr. Kaufman has provided all of the information of a textbook in a package that reads like an entertaining novel. I give this to all of my entrepreneur clients."

- Jeffrey D. Steed, Attorney at Law, Callister Nebeker & McCullough

"Having poor financial records is like getting on an airplane without knowing your destination. No one in their right mind would do this; however, people do this every day with their company finances. Financial records are the road map to success. Ken's book will teach you why great companies have great records.

-Jeff Jensen, CPA;
Principal, JAT Accounting & Tax

"As a small-business entrepreneur, accounting and finance are the areas I worry about most, but feel the least comfortable with. Ken Kaufman's remarkable book has somehow packed a college education and years of experience into an entertaining and comprehensible story that has given me a better understanding of my business and a new outlook on how to grow. *Impact Your Business* has a permanent place in my desktop reference library."

- Cary Snowden, President, Square Compass

"I wish all my clients would read *Impact Your Business*. I have seen far too many entrepreneurs and business owner's overestimate their abilities to understand business finance and accounting; and their efforts are often redundant, meaningless, and without strategic direction as a result. The entrepreneurs that embrace IMPACT will be able to financially see the results of their hard work and decisions. Certainly business owners will be able to more clearly forecast future plans. This book and the IMPACT model offer all business owners a complete dashboard to corporate finance."

David Gardner, VP, RCM Investments

"*Impact Your Business* is strongly practical in orientation. It quickly gets to the heart of issues that every entrepreneur faces and then systematically guides the reader through a program that helps entrepreneurs overcome challenges. With terrific insight and an easy-to-follow style, Ken has captured smart business principles that make sense. What's more is that he inspires the reader to put them to practice! I heartily endorse *Impact Your Business* for anyone interested in running a profit-disciplined business and finding time to be more effective in life!"

> - Matthew J. Hawkins, software business executive, Harvard Business School MBA; Father, husband, little league coach and a guy trying to find time to make it all happen!

"*Impact Your Business* is a read that all entrepreneurs can truly identify with. With an entertaining twist, Ken does a does a fabulous job articulating the true bedrock principles of finance that must be constantly evaluated and managed effectively by a business owner. The IMPACT insights offered throughout the book are key foundational points of a successful entrepreneur. Though not always easily identified by the individual they are an innate part that drives the success of a business."

> - Justin Long, Principal, Trizon, LLC

"This book is a MUST READ. *Impact Your Business* is a great tool for many of my clients and entrepreneurs everywhere."

> - Scott Miller, RHU; President, MillerWade Group

"Ken Kaufman is one of the business world's brightest minds. An entrepreneur, consultant, and author himself, he has created a method that allows talented CFOs to provide the application of financial data in day-to-day decision making of organizations. Having worked as an accounting professional, controller, CFO and COO for over 20 years, I have seen the ongoing challenge of providing IMPACT type indicators to upper management, executives, or the board who lack proper understanding and knowledge of how to apply financial information. Through Ken's IMPACT systems, no longer is there an excuse to not apply financial information to steer a company in a prosperous direction. Ken's allegory not only teaches us the value of having balance between family and career, but also illustrates how to apply financial information to resolve common challenges all company's face. The IMPACT application of financial information is not just left to the financially literate. Now non-accountant and non-finance educated owners and managers and professionals can reap the full benefits of the cost of their accounting systems."

> -Garth D. Allred, CEO, Furniture-Online.com

"*Impact Your Business* is a powerful read that simplifies and clarifies the aspect of business that scares most visionary entrepreneurs. I recommend Ken and his book to any business owner."

> - Jeff Rust, CEO, Corporate Alliance

"Finally, a book that makes financial verbiage easy to understand! Many entrepreneurs can create great companies because they have a great product or idea, but in the weeks, months and years down the road the numbers don't make sense and businesses fail. *Impact Your Business* is a light, easy read that will make you say, 'I get it!' What Ken Blanchard did to help managers by in *The One Minute Manager* series, Kaufman does to help entrepreneurs conquer the financial skeletons lurking in every office closet!"

-Michelle McCullough, Partner/Business Development Director, StartupPrincess.com

"Kaufman does an extraordinary job presenting practical financial principles in a clever and creative way. Every entrepreneur should have *Impact Your Business* as an essential financial handbook, and Kaufman's 44 Impact Insights should be posted in every office."

- Derek Miner, Co-Founder of OrangeSoda.com

"Regardless of your business model or industry, this book will have an impact on your business. Ken tells a story that every entrepreneur can relate to. It will open your eyes to the importance of clarity of purpose so you can focus on what's truly important in your business, and your life."

- Dave Bascom, GM Local Search, Deseret Digital Media

"*Impact Your Business* takes financial strategy from typical 'bore' to helping entrepreneurs 'score.' The allegory unfolded by the author is a fast read and I love the IMPACT Insights sprinkled throughout the story. Every business owner should read this book. Ken Kaufman gets it big time!"

- John Pilmer, Entrepreneur, Communications Pro and Author of the novel, *Green Spin*

IMPACT YOUR BUSINESS

An Allegory Of An Entrepreneur's Journey To
Clarity, Cash, Profit, Family, And Success

Ken Kaufman

Cover design by Jenevieve Hubbard of BlackBird Creative, www.blackbirdcreative.com

ISBN: 0-9831010-0-0
ISBN-13: 978-0983101000

First Edition

CFO WISE, INC.
PO BOX 516
Pleasant Grove, UT 84062, USA
www.CFOwise.com

To my father, for teaching me to work.
To my mother, for teaching me to play.
To my wife, whose talents and joie de vivre
Are my blessing to enjoy every day.

CONTENTS

INTRODUCTION

I want to forever change your perspective of accounting and finance. Most entrepreneurs, business owners, and executives I know equate listening to a presentation on or reading a book about these topics as a cure for insomnia. Truth be told, they're usually right.

But the numbers of a business, when used correctly, generate clarity. And clarity is the key to unlocking the potential of your business, your employees, and even you. Conversely, treating the accounting and finance elements of a company as an after-thought, or even disregarding them altogether, is hurting your business more than you may realize.

That's right, I'm suggesting most of the more than 25 million small and medium-sized businesses in the United States, and the millions of others around the world, are missing out. Just some of the reasons entrepreneurs shy away from accounting and finance, or the numbers side of business, include:

- It's complicated
- It's confusing
- It speaks a language all its own
- It requires a high degree of attention to detail and organization
- It's almost never beneficial for you or any other entrepreneur to become an expert in these areas

My purpose for this book is to teach you why you need to make

Introduction

accounting and finance a priority, how to do it without bogging yourself down in the details of it all, and how to cost effectively leverage it into helping you maximize your efforts in your venture. But I wrestled with how best to share this information without it being viewed as boring, non-value-added, and, therefore, incorrectly disregarded or discounted.

So I decided to write most of this book in a fictional novel format. It will entertain while it educates as you follow the roller coaster ride of just one entrepreneur whose business and family are on the brink of ruin. Although difficult, he transitions to getting the information and data he needs to run and improve his business, and he learns to assimilate and interpret that information to make the most of his entrepreneurial efforts. His transition includes learning about and implementing the six scoreboards every business needs, all of which adhere to the IMPACT criteria explained throughout the book.

But this isn't just a fictional group of people and events. It's an allegory, which means all of the main characters and elements of the story are symbols to which we can easily relate, yet they represent something of greater depth and significance. Here's a brief introduction to the symbols, with a complete list of explanations in the glossary at the end of the book.

Please meet Steve Loveland. He is the amalgamation of all the business owners and entrepreneurs I have or will ever know. Steve is the main character in the allegory, which makes him the main symbol. He represents all of us who have or will ever start, operate, or run a small to medium-sized business.

His family represents the most important thing in his life. Maybe it really is your family, or maybe it's something else for you. Whatever it is, Steve is guilty of neglecting it for the sake of his entrepreneurial baby.

Steve's going to face some tough challenges that almost destroy his business and his life. These challenges represent the challenges you face every day in your business. They can be solved, just like Steve's.

Steve gets exactly the help he needs from Jennifer Silverstone. Jennifer represents the top-caliber finance executives who have foregone corporate America to help the rising generation of entrepreneurs. They provide Chief Financial Officer (CFO) services that are revolutionizing the way small and medium-sized businesses can affordably access the serious financial firepower they need to be more competitive and more effectively attain their goals and objectives.

This is not a book that talks about theory and falls short of helping you implement its principles, concepts, and teachings. After the allegory, please keep reading the last three sections of the book. These sections include a more in-depth explanation of the Concepts taught by the allegory along with How-To detail and additional Tools and Resources to help you make the IMPACT transition in your business. These three sections also include plenty of examples from various industries and sizes of businesses.

In addition, I have and will continue to add tools, information, and resources to our website for your reference and use. At the back of this book you will find the website address as well as a code to grant you free access to over $350 worth of information and resources, including an industry analysis and data report for your specific company.

Now, let's get started with the story so you can start applying its principles and *Impact Your Business*.

The Allegory

1

BOTTOM

Steve glared out his office window at the far corner of the building. Black storm clouds cast shadows, like threatening competitors on his faltering business, onto the snow-capped mountain range. The forty Bolty Solutions employees had left an hour earlier. He usually looked forward to the peace and quiet of an empty office, but not today. He chuckled at the irony. How could he enjoy any tranquility in the office when he didn't have enough money to pay the rent?

How am I going to survive this mess, Steve wondered as he shuffled through the disorganized piles of paper on his desk. *Maybe if I clean up this works pace people around here won't have reason to believe Bolty's in as much trouble as we actually are.* He picked up a sheet of paper, another bill, with huge red letters 'PAST DUE' stamped across the middle.

When he started his business twelve years earlier, he thought being self-employed would be the best and last gig he ever had. How was he going to turn the company around? How had things gone so wrong so quickly?

The ugly past due bill was from his bank. He had obtained a loan almost a year earlier when Bolty began to encounter cash flow shortages. Now he was one month behind on that loan. As he tossed the bill onto one of the biggest of the piles, he fingered the next document, a letter from the IRS. Thanks to a recent audit, he now owed the government a significant amount of back-taxes, penalties, and interest.

Steve kept sifting the papers around, hoping to find a positive spin to his difficult situation. *There must be something good here.* His head ached as his paper-shuffling became more desperate. But the next sheet was even worse, detailing the lawsuit in which he and Bolty were recently named.

No matter what I do, I just can't seem to get ahead. Steve dropped the papers and sank back into his chair. *If only I could have convinced Intermountain Engineering to stay with us rather than take their projects to our competitor. My two best programmers quit last week – I'll bet my competitor, TRM Programming, hires them.* His perspective darkened with each negative thought, like the sky as the storm settled in. He closed his eyes, rested his elbows on the desk and his head in his hands, and felt the shadows outside fill his office and saturate his mind.

How could this happen to me? That gave Steve an idea. He found a pen and pad under one of the looming stacks and wrote 'Timeline' on the top of the page. Perhaps this would help him put things in perspective. Underneath it he drew a horizontal line and put twelve equidistant tick marks on the line, one for each year of the company's life.

He skipped to the sixth year and wrote 'booming economy, great income.' That was the year things really came together. Back then he struggled to hire talented programmers fast enough to keep up with the demand. *I was making a lot of money then. If only the economy hadn't tanked in year nine.*

We shouldn't have bought that huge house. How am I going to tell Aubrye we might go out of business? I can't find a job in this recession. And if I found one, it would never pay enough for us to keep our newly-acquired lifestyle and put away enough money for college for all four kids.

Steve rubbed his temples, and he could feel his receding hairline. He threw his hands up in the air, leaned back, and said out loud, "It's time to give up." Shame filled him.

From the corner of his eye he saw the digital clock on the wall and panic shot through his body. *Oh no, Tyler is going to kill me. And I'm going to get another lecture from Aubrye about being an absentee parent of our four children and the additional burdens that puts on her.*

Steve hurriedly put his laptop and a few thick files in his bag, locked the door, and began the commute. Rush hour had long since passed, but traffic on I-15, Salt Lake City's main freeway, was still moving slowly thanks to the freshly-fallen snow. The storm had passed, but he knew he would be walking into another one as soon as he got home.

2
REJECTION

Steve watched the garage door close in his rearview mirror. He dreaded the two inevitable confrontations he was about to have. *Tyler is so excited about his new learner's permit and he can't wait to get some driving time in. I guess I have to face him and his mom so I can see how upset they are with me.*

From the garage, Steve walked through the laundry room and into the kitchen, the brightest room in the house. Aubrye stood at the sink on the far wall, rinsing dishes. She wore the floral-patterned apron the kids bought her for Mother's Day last year, and her dark brown hair reached to the small of her back.

"You promised Tyler you would go with him, and now it's too late." Aubrye piled the dinner plates in the dishwasher, then clanged some pots into the sink. "You're sending a very clear message that you care more about that business than your own family. He really needs you right now, and the more you let him down, the more he'll pull away from us."

"I had to stop working just to make it home now, and I am still buried." Steve's defensive tone overpowered his tired voice.

Aubrye set a dish down and reached for a towel to dry her hands while turning toward Steve. Her long hair followed her movement and fell perfectly into place. Her blue eyes expressed disappointment. "If this was the first time you failed to keep a commitment, then I would likely buy that story. But I'm not even going to respond to that excuse, and I doubt Tyler will either."

Steve approached his wife. "I'm sorry."

Aubrye put her right hand out, stopping Steve in his tracks. "You know what happened the last time I took Tyler driving with all of the kids. He became so distracted with the commotion they were causing he almost plowed into the back of a semi. I need you to either watch the younger kids or take him driving; I just can't do both."

"I'll go and talk to Tyler. I just can't seem to win today." Steve was hoping for sympathy.

"Good luck. He's secluded himself to his room, no doubt entrenched in one of those video games." Aubrye began to finish the last few dishes.

Steve thought back to six years earlier when things at Bolty really started to come together, the year after their youngest, Emma, was born. With his salary, the profit from the business, and Aubrye's salary, they were making very good money. They no longer needed Aubrye's income to sustain themselves. Although a tenured professor at the local University, she had longed to spend more time with the kids before they grew up and were gone. Aubrye left a job she loved for kids she loved even more, comfortable Steve's income would either stay the same or continue to improve.

For Aubrye to be that upset with me, she must really be at the end of her patience. She doesn't normally react with so much frustration toward me. Steve pulled out his iPhone and began texting while ascending the stairs. In an effort to warm his son up to a face-to-face conversation, he resorted to his son's favorite medium of communication.

Feeling like the failure his wife had just made him out to be, Steve texted: Tyler, I'm sorry. Can we talk?

Steve could almost feel his son's frustration and anger through the cellular air waves when he received this message in response: no. how about I 4get u asked, like u 4got 2 take me driving 2night?

Preferring any response to the silent treatment, Steve took confidence that Tyler might actually talk to him. Steve knocked on Tyler's door.

"Dad, you totally know I need you to go driving with me for like a million hours before I can get my license. You've been promising me we could go for the last two weeks, and we haven't even gone once yet."

Through the door Steve implored, "Tyler, I know I let you down. Is there any way you would consider letting your slacker father come in?"

"All right."

Steve opened the door to reveal a typical teenage boy's room. The last four days of clothing were strewn across the floor, the bed was a mixture of sheets, blankets, and popcorn remains. Vibrant posters of favorite athletes covered the walls. Tyler leaned back in a chair, holding a video game controller in his hands, his big, bare feet perched on a small table where the game console and a small monitor sat.

Steve was a little surprised at Tyler's respectful gesture of removing his earphones when he turned to look at his father, although he failed to part the long, black hair that covered his green eyes. "Look, I've been under a lot of pressure lately, but that's no excuse for not keeping my promises to you. Is there any way I can make it right?"

Tyler rolled his eyes. "You seriously want me to try and figure out how you can make it right. It's simple. Forget about that dumb business just long enough to take me driving."

"How about tomorrow night, then?"

"I've got a basketball game tomorrow night. Man, I think I'm going to be the only kid in my whole school without a driver's license. Just forget about it." Tyler turned back to the game, plugged his earphones in, and resumed play.

Deflated, Steve went back downstairs to the kitchen. Aubrye was waiting for him, and she seemed much more melancholy than normal. "Your business is ruining all of our lives."

Steve had heard this lecture before, and he was not in the mood to hear it again. "Do you think I have some magic wand to wave at all of our problems to make them just disappear? I'm trying, and things are getting worse, not better."

"Well, all I know is things in this family were better when that business was doing better. You had more time to spend with us. I'm not trying to harp on you. But the kids need you. I miss you. I didn't quit working for a family life like this." Aubrye began to cry. "I'm so tired. I just can't keep up with everything by myself."

Steve felt the muscles in his shoulders tighten. "And I can't keep up with the business. I'm overwhelmed."

Aubrye's tears flowed more freely. "You see, this is the problem. You're obsessed with that company. The worse it has gotten, the more you've pulled away from us."

Aubrye wiped her cheeks with her shirt sleeve. "It seems like the only way to get you to be involved with this family again is to get that business fixed. You can't seem to find time for us when it's broken, so you better fix it, and fast."

Aubrye untied her apron and hung it on the hook next to the refrigerator. She walked to the bottom of the stairs where she stopped, her shaking hand resting on the banister. Without turning around, she spoke in a tone dripping with despondence. "Looks like I'll be going to bed alone again tonight. I'm sure you have plenty of work to keep you busy." She slogged up the stairs to their bedroom.

She's right – I'm going to stay up late working. I have to. If I don't save my company, no one else will. Bolty may very well fail before she gives up on me, anyway. I love Aubrye. She's means so much to me, and it's killing me that I'm hurting her so much right now.

He walked through the kitchen and opened the door to his home office. The dimly-lit room was a stark contrast to the bright kitchen and resembled a cave, a place where he could hibernate until all of this blew over. *Maybe I should shut the business down and become a caveman,* he thought with bitterness.

Slumping into his chair, Steve's thoughts sunk lower than he'd ever allowed himself to go. *I really am a huge failure. My life is falling apart and I can't seem to do anything right to fix it. My wife thinks I'm a loser, and she's not cutting me much slack any more. I'm going to crack under all of this stress. I need just a little more time to figure all of this out.*

Moving from his chair, he dropped down into an old leather couch in the far corner of the room. Trying to be positive he mumbled to the dark room, *I just don't think things can get any worse.*

Due to the result of many sleepless nights in the last weeks and his total exhaustion from yet another altercation with Aubrye, he fell asleep and didn't wake until morning, his dreams filled with panicky images of his family leaving, carrying suitcases in their hands.

3
PAYROLL

Steve awoke early the next morning, awkwardly smashed onto the uncomfortable couch in his home office. *Wow, my neck sure is stiff and my right arm is completely asleep.* He sat up and gathered his senses. The newly-risen sun poured brilliant light into the neatly-kept room. *Just early enough to grab a quick shower and leave for work before anyone wakes up. I don't want to face the same wrath I did last night.*

Just twenty minutes later Steve stood in front of the downstairs bathroom mirror, running his fingers through his thinning black hair. With weary fingers he placed contacts over his brown eyes. After slipping into the garage and starting his car, he pulled out and noticed several inches of snow on the driveway. *Aubrye probably wants me to shovel this, but I have so much work to do I can't take the time right now. I needed to catch up last night, but instead I let myself fall asleep on that old, uncomfortable couch. I'm too tired and busy to face another fight, or all this snow shoveling. Wish I could count on Tyler to help out, but little chance of that.*

Like every morning drive to the office for the last several months, Steve felt sick to his stomach. He was in over his head, and nothing he was doing seemed to make it any better. The salt and sand left by the snowplows from the night before created a thin, mucky film that covered the roads and every car driving on them.

Steve pulled into an almost empty parking lot and noted Judy's car in its usual spot. Judy Duke was one of his first hires after starting the business. She had become a trusted and loyal office manager, great at keeping track of details and managing some of the day-to-day issues that would otherwise distract Steve from growing and now trying to save the business.

The interior of Steve's heated car was a stark contrast to the brisk cold he felt as he exited and walked to the building. He opened the large glass door and entered the attractive, professional lobby. A tall counter with a receptionist desk sat in the middle of the marble floor with a large, walnut door to the right--the passageway to the inner-workings of Bolty.

As Steve walked through that door, he remembered renting this space. Its impressive lobby and the efficient layout of the rest of the office-- one large rectangular room with a few dozen tall-walled cubicles in the middle and several offices and conference rooms around the perimeter-- would certainly send a message that Bolty was successful. *What a joke that turned out to be.*

He made his way to the far corner office, opened the door, set his bag on one of the leather chairs in front of his desk, and then sunk into his oversized, black leather executive chair.

Within a minute, a light knock on his office door was followed by Judy sticking her head through the doorway, her blonde hair pulled back in a bun. "Hey Boss. We have a problem. Can we talk?" Her hazel eyes were more tired than normal and Steve could hear stress in her voice.

"Sure." Steve wondered if staying on the couch at home may have been a better choice.

Judy stepped into his office and pulled the door closed behind her. She tilted her head downward, looking at Steve over the top rim of her glasses. "Do you remember when we had that conversation a few months ago about payroll? You know, the one where I should come and let you know if we don't have enough cash to pay everyone."

"Yes, I do." Steve sighed. *Here it comes.*

Judy sat down in the chair just next to the one where Steve had placed his bag. "Well, we're there. Payday is today and we only have $60,000 to cover it."

"Total payroll is just over $80,000, right?" Steve knew the answer, but hoped he might be wrong.

"Yes." Judy's single word answer sounded innocent but was as catastrophic as a bomb. She straightened her shoulders, looking away from Steve. He wondered how she could look so pulled together and even happy, since he knew she was struggling with issues of her own. She had told him several months earlier that her husband was seriously injured while riding an ATV and how grateful she was for the good insurance Bolty provided. So far he hadn't been able to return to work, making Judy the sole bread-winner for her family.

Steve's mind reeled. "Judy, how did we get into this mess? More importantly, how are we going to get out? Is there any other place where we can free up some short term cash?"

Judy shifted in her chair, her shoulders suddenly slumping and her soft, kind features looking almost haggard. Though she just turned fifty, she might be mistaken for 65 at that moment. *What am I doing to everyone in my life?*

Steve recalled several conversations through the years about how she would do anything for the company but accounting and finance were not her strongest points, especially when it came to trying to creatively maneuver resources to handle cash flow crunches.

In a subdued, almost defeated voice, Judy answered, "I don't know of any. Our line of credit is tapped out. I've spoken with several customers the last few days, and they all promise to pay us next week, which will be too late."

"OK. Let me think about it and let's reconvene before lunch. We're going to get through this, Judy." Steve stood up, his signature method for letting his employees know he was done with the conversation.

Judy stood and headed toward the door. Steve noticed her tennis shoes and jeans, reminding him it was Friday--casual day. He wished he had remembered that earlier to avoid getting his newly pressed navy blue dress pants from the closet, almost waking his wife. Judy stopped and looked back. "For what it's worth, I think we don't have enough work to support our staffing levels. We're doing less work than we were two years ago and we still have about the same number of employees. Seems like we could save some money there."

Steve took a moment before he answered. "Yeah, I've had the same thought, but what about the way we've raised our prices to account for the increased complexity of most of our projects? It seems like that should offset the decrease in work."

"Maybe you can't afford me anymore." Judy's tone was quiet and even.

Shocked by her suggestion, Steve gathered his thoughts for another moment. "I'm not sure I'm comfortable with what you're suggesting, Judy. Where did that come from?"

"This company has been struggling for a long time and it has taken a toll on me." Judy's voice and face became more animated. "I'll have to be the one to tell everyone they aren't getting a paycheck after I've been assuring them that the company is fine. It seems easier to quit rather than face them."

"Hey, we have until this afternoon when you normally hand out the paychecks to figure this out. I think we can pull this off. Do you disagree?"

Judy squinted her eyes and shrugged her shoulders. "Kind of. For months we've been getting closer and closer to not making payroll. It's getting worse, not better."

"Judy, you know how much I value you as part of this company. You've done so much for me through the years. I don't want you to have to tell everyone they are not getting paid. Give me a little time to get my head around this and then we'll circle back by noon. Okay?"

IMPACT INSIGHT #1

Entrepreneurs carry great optimism toward their ventures, even when it seems like they should have no hope.

"Okay." Judy left the door half-open. Steve sat back down in his chair and swiveled to look out his favorite window. The snowfall from the night before left a beautiful white blanket on the mountains, making him wish he could get a similar fresh start to his day and his business.

This might be the beginning of the end. If I can't make payroll, I'll surely lose my key people, and then my business will crumble.

4
MEETING

Steve contemplated his dire situation longer than he intended, dwelling on his two newest problems--not enough cash for payroll and his tenured office manager wanting to quit. Judy's voice through the phone pulled him from his hopelessness. "Jennifer Silverstone is here to see you."

Judy must be covering the phones until the receptionist arrives in another half hour. "Send her back," he muttered as he wrung his hands together, as if to wash himself of the anxiety that had been mounting since the night before. He stood to greet his guest.

Within seconds, the door, already half-open, swung open to reveal a brown-haired woman, probably in her early forties. Her dark gray jacket and slacks matched Steve's current mood.

"Hello," the woman said gregariously. "I'm Jennifer Silverstone, and I'm here for our appointment." Ms. Silverstone extended her hand in a businesslike manner, which adequately described her outward appearance-- professional and competent. But the slight smile in the right corner of her mouth and her kind green eyes made her seem like a friend.

As he shook her hand, Steve tried desperately to replace feelings of despondence and failure with confidence and vision--a facade he had practiced a lot during the past year, but he knew it wouldn't last long. He was a lousy actor, along with everything else these days.

"Hello, Jennifer. I'm Steve Loveland. Please have a seat." Steve gestured toward the two leather chairs in front of his desk. He saw one of the chairs occupied by his work bag and pointed to the empty chair. "That chair is fine."

"That sounds great. Thanks." Jennifer's voice was friendly and enthusiastic, maybe a little too much so. She sat down and crossed her legs. She pulled an iPad from her bag and placed it on her lap while Steve stepped around his desk, picked up his bag with a jerk, and moved it next to his chair on the floor. He sat down as Jennifer leaned forward slightly, looking at Steve with an energetic eagerness. Steve wasn't sure if it was annoying or impressive.

Steve sighed. *The last thing I need is an over-zealous know-it-all consultant with lots of degrees and letters behind her name who can quote every textbook about why my business is struggling but has no idea how to actually fix it.*

Steve felt trapped, like when he wants to be alone, sitting around in sweats watching a ball game, but his wife forces him to attend a social event where he's supposed to try and be nice and interested in people he could care less about. *I need to tell this lady that there is no chance for her or anyone else to resuscitate my business.* Instead he pulled his laptop from its bag, placed it in its usual spot in the middle of his desk, and attached it to a power cord and Ethernet cable.

Other than the gentle hum of his laptop starting up, Steve's office was silent as he waited for Jennifer to speak. "Jeff Hanks called me last week and suggested I reach out to you. He failed to mention how the two of you know each other."

Grateful to talk about a subject other than his host of failures, Steve thought back to the first time he and Jeff were introduced. "Jeff and I met several years ago when I was his assistant coach for our sons' basketball team. His son, Tim, is the same age as my son, Tyler. I've grown to respect his judgment and opinion. That's probably the only reason I was willing to take your call."

"You certainly could have hung up on me." Jennifer smiled. "It seems like you have built a successful company here at Bolty."

Something inside Steve snapped. He was fed up with the word 'successful'. *What are the criteria to be called that, anyway? I'm the furthest thing from being successful. There's no use hiding it. I'm just going to tell her the truth.*

"You know, I've never felt less successful in all of my life." His voice was full of fatigue and uncertainty. "I have some serious problems and I just don't know how to overcome any of them. I think my business is about to fall apart." Steve lowered his head, unable to meet Jennifer's pleasant gaze. "My family isn't too far behind."

"Is this why Jeff wanted us to meet?" Jennifer stroked her shoulder-length hair behind her ears with her hands.

"Yes, I'm sure it is." Steve re-situated himself in his chair, hoping to chase away the feeling of having shared too much. "He said you know how to help people like me."

"Well, I don't know if I can help yet, but I have some questions about you and your business. Tell me how you got started."

Steve looked at his incomplete timeline from the night before. "My start goes back to my college days at Pepperdine University in Malibu, California. I worked part-time for IntegraTech Manufacturing while going to school, and then I worked for them full-time after I graduated. We made electrical and other technology-based parts for electronic and computer devices. Our customers were some of the largest companies in the world."

Steve ran his finger across his laptop's track pad and the screen came to life. He wished reviving his business was as simple. He was surprised that he genuinely wanted to share his story--at least partially so he could mentally complete his timeline. He put his index finger on the first tick-mark. "I moved here to Utah to run a company called Intermountain Production Services, or IPS, after IntegraTech purchased it. Unbeknownst to IntegraTech, IPS was in big trouble and collapsed just six months later. That's when I started Bolty."

Jennifer awoke her iPad and began typing notes on the touch screen. "So you woke up one morning and you were an entrepreneur, launching your own business. Is that right?"

"Yes, kind of a weird twist of fate, don't you think?" Steve raised his eyebrows.

Jennifer carefully slid her arms out of the sleeves of her jacket while balancing the iPad on her lap, revealing a firmly pressed white blouse. "Well, it depends on how you look at it. Although the details always differ, I think most people start their own businesses from relatively similar circumstances – not happy with where they are and who they're with so they launch into their own venture."

15

> **IMPACT INSIGHT #2**
> *Most people start businesses because it's their best option, not because they have a product or service that will take over the world.*

Steve pondered that, then realized he had dominated the conversation more than he intended. "Jennifer, I've told you a lot about me, maybe too much. In fact, I've been more honest about my situation with you than almost anyone else. I think it is your turn now. Tell me what I should know about you."

The tech-savvy visitor finished typing. "I earned my undergrad and MBA here in Utah. I've held several management and executive positions with larger companies, and once with a small business. Five years ago, I decided to focus on helping several companies at a time, none of which needed me on a full-time basis. I think that was the best career move I've ever made."

Steve leaned forward like a patient, hoping to receive a clean bill of health. "Why is that?"

"There are lots of reasons. The main one is that I've found that many business owners and entrepreneurs find themselves in a position not too dissimilar to yours."

Somehow Steve took comfort in hearing he was part of a larger group. *I bet I'm the biggest failure of them all though*, he thought with irony. "I'm hoping they all didn't go out of business." Steve tried to appear confident but suspected he sounded anxious, even desperate. "Did they all survive?"

"Some do and some don't, from my experience." Jennifer spoke with ease and eloquence, every word making her seem more professional and polished. "But there are definitely some common themes among those who pull out of their downward spiral and get their businesses back on track – well, one theme in particular."

"I'm curious. What is it?" Steve wanted to know, hoping for a 'silver-bullet' recipe to save his business.

"In a nutshell, it has to do with a difficult transition all businesses must endure if they want to grow into a genuine, going concern that does not require the business owner's full-time attention to every detail."

IMPACT INSIGHT #3

To grow beyond the point where the owner is involved in every detail of the business, every business must make a transition.

Jennifer's words resonated with Steve and he leaned back in his chair. Then he remembered not being able to make payroll and began to panic, imagining all of the people he might have to lay off, maybe as soon as that afternoon. "Jennifer, have you ever helped companies who are having serious cash flow issues?"

5
PROJECT

Jennifer lowered her eyebrows and tilted her head slightly. "I'm not sure I understand your question. What did you mean when you asked if I've ever helped companies with serious cash flow issues?"

Steve ran his right index finger along the edge of his desk, embarrassed he was going to reveal how bad off his business really was. "Have you ever helped a company when they were running out of cash?"

Jennifer's expression returned to normal. "Quite often." Steve was interested that she seemed neither surprised nor judgmental.

Steve's eyes followed his finger as he continued to stroke it back and forth along the edge of the desk while he mulled over his next statement. "OK. I have an idea. How would you like to help me with a little project this morning?" Steve asked.

"I would be very open to that." Jennifer paused for a moment. "But in my experience most 'little' projects that have to do with cash flow issues usually turn into big projects."

"The reality is that I have a serious problem I need to try and fix today, and nobody in my company knows how to solve it. Jeff said he has trusted you with his business, so I'm relying on his recommendation. If you or someone like you can't help me, my company will likely not survive. I really have nothing to lose." Steve tensed and hoped he didn't sound like he was begging. *My little sales pitch sounds pretty desperate. But I am desperate. No use in hiding it.* He sighed.

Jennifer glanced down at her iPad, then back at Steve. "I'm always up for a challenge. I'm in, but I can only stay for a few hours."

"How much will it cost to get you on such short notice?" Steve held his breath.

Jennifer looked at the ceiling, then back at Steve. "How about I help this morning for no cost--almost like a test drive? If you like the results, and if it looks like you're going to survive, then we can figure out if it makes sense to continue to work together. Deal?"

"No cost always works for me, but hopefully I get more than I pay for." Steve smiled, forcing himself to lighten the mood and hopefully feel less ashamed of the mess he was in.

"You should be less worried about the value I will bring and more worried about how much it is going to cost after this freebie."

Steve raised his hands in the air. "Touché."

"Since this is a cash problem that needs to be fixed immediately, I'm going to guess this little project has something to do with your largest cash outflow--your employees. Is payroll due today?"

"Wow, how did you know that?" As Steve asked the question, he realized the answer. "Oh yeah, you see pitiful companies like mine all the time."

The room suddenly seemed much quieter. After at least ten seconds, Steve finally spoke. "My office manager, Judy, who you met at the reception desk, informed me before you arrived we're $20,000 shy of paying everyone. I want you to see if you can help us make payroll."

The business woman uncrossed her legs and scooted to the edge of her chair, as though she was preparing to stand up. "I will need some time with Judy. Can you call her in so we can get started?"

The CEO pressed speakerphone and dialed the front desk extension. "Yes," Judy answered.

"Judy, can you please come to my office?" Steve's voice was smooth, masking the panic he felt. "I've got an idea on solving our payroll situation. Jennifer, who's right here with me, is going to help. Can you come to my office?"

"Sure thing," Judy replied.

Jennifer stood up and turned toward the door. Judy entered, her glasses hanging around her neck. Jennifer extended her hand to the office manager. "Hi, Judy, I'm Jennifer Silverstone. We met briefly when I came in

20

this morning."

"Hello." Judy shook her hand, looking at Steve for direction.

Steve quickly scrambled for the right words. "Judy, Jennifer comes highly recommended by a good friend of mine. She helps companies like ours on a regular basis. I've asked her to work with you to see if we can free up any cash for payroll. Please give her access to everything she needs."

Judy nodded, then looked at Jennifer with the usual skepticism she always had toward newcomers.

Jennifer picked up her things. "Judy, I have a bunch of questions for you, and I'll bet you'll be able to answer them best from your desk. Would it be alright if we go there?"

"Okay." Steve heard some reservation in Judy's voice. He realized she cared about the company almost as much as he did. He was humbled by her loyalty. *I've gotta make things better. So many people are depending on me.*

"I'll be back to you by 11:30." Carrying her bag and jacket, Jennifer followed Judy out Steve's door.

Steve hoped Jennifer was more than an appealing idea that was far from being able to actually help his company. *This had better work.* He sat back in his chair and turned his focus to his email inbox on his laptop. I guess I'll know in a few hours.

6
CASH

The sun outside was melting the snowfall from yesterday, similar to the way Steve was reducing his delinquent workload that morning. He finished off a few lingering proposals, replied to several dozen emails, and made phone calls to prospects and customers.

The sick feeling in his stomach lingered as doubts about Bolty's survival made him question if his company would be around long enough to do the projects he was chasing.

"Are you ready for me?" Jennifer stood in Steve's office doorway.

Steve motioned with his right hand for Jennifer to come in. "You're early. I hope that means you have good news."

Jennifer sat in the same chair she did earlier. "Some good and bad news. Which do you want first?"

The nausea in Steve's stomach intensified. "I need as much good as you can offer me. Good news first, please."

Jennifer obliged. "The good news is that we've freed up about $25,000 of cash flow, so you'll be able to make payroll."

"That's great!" Steve blurted and a few employees in the cubicles just outside his closed office door jerked their heads up to look his way. Steve lowered his voice a bit. "How did you do it?"

"I went through all of your cash outflows for the past three months and realized that Judy was paying most of your vendors too early. She and I corrected that and found a few other ways to positively impact your working capital cycle immediately."

IMPACT INSIGHT #4

Many entrepreneurial companies can manage their cash flow more efficiently than they currently are by maximizing what is referred to as the working capital cycle.

"Really? I thought Judy had things more under control than that."

"She follows a great process, but it's not uncommon for office managers in her position to make choices that actually hurt cash flow. It's certainly not intentional, but it usually makes their jobs easier, eliminating phone calls from vendors looking for money." Jennifer smoothed her gray wool dress pants.

Steve's relief was swallowed by Jennifer's smile disappearing from her face. "So, tell me the bad news. How bad is it?"

Jennifer cleared her throat and straightened in her seat. "The bad news is that finding these cash inefficiencies is a one-time help to cash flow. Skipping vendor payments will help this week, but then those payments must be made every week thereafter. It will get us through this valley, but now that we've used it up, we can't draw on it again. There's something else causing more permanent challenges, and I have a hunch I know what it is."

IMPACT INSIGHT #5

Making working capital more efficient is only a one-time help to cash flow. A company that still has cash shortages after working capital is maximized almost always has bigger problems.

"So, what's causing the problem?" Steve was rigid, a mountain made of granite.

"It looks like our payroll is too high relative to the volume of work we have. I think we may need to right-size our staff." Jennifer lowered her hands from making quotation marks around 'right-size.'

"And by right-size, you mean lay people off, right?" Steve closed his eyes and put his head in his hands, awash with defeat.

"Yes. But I'm not sure how much we need to cut. I'll need a little more time to figure it out."

Jennifer's words hit Steve like a large truck slamming into a steel-reinforced brick wall. He was hoping to avoid this, but he could run from it no more. "How much more time?"

"Probably another day of working with Judy and doing some additional analysis." Jennifer folded her hands in her lap, a gesture that somehow convinced Steve she really understood his dismay and distress.

"Shoot! I have to wait this out over the weekend?" Steve's hands tightened to fists, and tension filled his entire body.

IMPACT INSIGHT #6
Entrepreneurs usually like to make decisions quickly, but they can often benefit by waiting an extra couple of days for better information.

"This is a critical decision with broad implications. We need to be sure before we take action." Jennifer was like a war general trying to steady her failing troops. "I want to look at all our options. The question is how deep do we need to cut, and will it be deep enough to get us back on track without compromising our business."

Jennifer checked her iPhone. "I can be back Monday afternoon--one o'clock. Will that work?"

"Yes, this is my top priority. I will make it work." Steve's defeat was a weight on his heart. For the millionth time he asked himself, *how could I have let things get this bad?*

Jennifer took a breath. "We will also need to discuss my fees on Monday."

"Well, it's obvious I need your help and advice. Shoot, if you can make cash appear like you just did for payroll, I think I might even be able to pay you." Again Steve tried to dismiss his stress and shame with a little humor.

Jennifer broke a small smile. "Steve, there is still some tough terrain ahead--difficult decisions and painful changes."

"Hopefully not as painful as the last 24 hours." Steve shook his head. "I want you to help me."

"I'd like to help. I'll see you on Monday. I really need to leave for my next meeting."

"OK. Enjoy your weekend." *Yours will be better than mine*, he wanted to add, thinking of all the families he was about to let down. Including his own.

Steve watched Jennifer return to Judy's office where the two spoke briefly. Jennifer handed Judy a business card, gathered her things, and left.

Steve walked to Judy's office and leaned against the doorway. "So, what did you think of her?"

Judy glanced up from her computer and gave a pleasant grin, still holding Jennifer's card in her hand. Steve had seen that look from Judy before, the one that very few people earned from her. "She really is quite good at what she does. She cut right to the chase and, quite honestly, got us out of a tough jam." Judy's face changed from smile to concern. "I feel a little bad that I was part of the problem."

"Did she make you feel that way?" Steve felt a little like a protective father.

"Actually, no. She was quite complimentary of my work, especially considering that I have no formal training or experience in accounting, other than what I have learned working for you."

"She's going to come back Monday at one to help us some more. Would you be all right with that?" Steve wasn't really asking for permission, but wanted Judy to know what was going to happen.

"I'm fine with it, as long as we can afford to pay her." Judy clasped her hands together. "I still think we need to be letting people go, not hiring more."

Steve walked all the way into her office and shut the door. He folded his arms. "Jennifer actually feels the same way. She's going to help us figure out how much we need to cut."

Judy's eyes widened as her mouth fell open. She looked like she wanted to say something, but nothing came out. *Oh, why did I say that to her. Now she's going to freak out about this all weekend. With two teenagers and a recently disabled husband to support, she needs her job now more than ever.*

Steve tried to settle her concerns. "I'm not trying to ruin your weekend but our close call with payroll and the advice from both of you has me convinced that we need to change some things--what we're doing isn't working. Of course, you know I'll welcome any of your thoughts on this as we get to the decision-making phase."

> **IMPACT INSIGHT #7**
> *Sometimes it takes the perspective of someone from outside the company to help an entrepreneur realize they need to make changes.*

"Is my name on the list?" Judy sounded like a vulnerable sailboat about to take on a category five hurricane.

"Judy, there's no list. Not yet, anyway."

Steve walked to Judy's desk and placed his left hand on the corner. "You've been with me longer than any other employee--and it's going to stay that way. Please don't stress out about it. We're going to put a plan together next week."

Judy gasped for air, having held her breath since her question. "Okay," was all she could muster. Steve didn't want to dwell on this topic any more.

As he walked back to his office he worried, *who are we going to let go?* His employees in their sea of cubicles worked steadily, loyally. With more regret than he could handle, he knew he would have to sacrifice some to save the rest. He'd avoided thinking about a layoff for months.

I'll need to get feedback from my managers through the weekend on how all of their employees are doing. Then I'll need to make a list, ordered by who I should let go first. With all of the other proposals to review and quality checks I'm doing on the current projects, it's going to be a long weekend.

Rather than return to his chair, Steve walked to his window as his thoughts turned to his failures at home. *If I can just get this business under control, I know things at home will improve. If the business fails, then my family will fail, too. Aubrye won't want to stay with someone who's a failure. Maybe she and the kids would be better off without me. But I can't stand the thought of losing them. As frustrating as Aubrye is right now, I still love her. I have to save the business, and that will save my family.*

From his stance at the window, Steve doubted his ability to improve his business or his family. He was hopeless, his default state of late.

7
TESTIMONIAL

Tyler's basketball game that night was another event Steve wished he could avoid. *But this is what good fathers do, right? Besides, maybe attending the game will keep Aubrye from getting upset with me--again.* The gym was chilly and unwelcoming, just like how Aubrye was treating him, as they sat together on the aluminum benches, surrounded by their three kids, who were bored, fretful, and demanding.

"Why don't you make yourself useful and take Emma to the bathroom?" Aubrye's voice was tired as she pushed the seven-year-old's hand into his.

The two plunked down the bleachers to the freshly finished wood gym floor while Steve thought about his wife. *She is bothered with me all the time, but it didn't use to be this way. I'm letting her down in so many ways.*

Steve reflected on the decision they had made several years earlier for her to quit her job as a professor at the local University so she could spend more time with the kids before they were grown and gone. Bolty was producing a great income, so it seemed like the right decision at the time. *If Bolty fails, maybe I'll need to stay home so she can go back to work. I'm sure the University would take her back in a heartbeat.*

Emma danced her way to the women's room, Steve weaving her between lots of families who seemed to be getting along and enjoying, not hating, their time together. Guilt welled in his gut.

"Dad, can we get some licorice at the snack bar." Emma looked up at Steve like a puppy hoping for scraps from the table.

"Okay, but let's take care of this bathroom trip first."

Seven-year-old Emma's black hair bounced on her back as she let go of Steve's hand and skipped to the bathroom entrance. *Her mom's blue eyes are so beautiful, so innocent. I hope with her fun personality she never ends up in the fix I'm in.*

Emma entered the restroom while Steve leaned his right shoulder against the cool, rough cinder block construction of the building's wall.

"Hey Loveland!" came a boisterous voice from behind Steve. He turned around to see Jeff Hanks wearing the opposing team's blue and white shirt, emblazoned with the Bingham Miners logo, a burly miner holding a pick.

They shook hands. "I'm not sure if I'm supposed to be friends with the enemy." Steve laughed, but it sounded weak, almost desperate.

"Yeah, it's too bad Tim and Tyler aren't going to the same high school." Jeff pushed the rim of his baseball cap up slightly, revealing more thick, sandy hair. "We sure had some fun coaching them when they were younger."

"Yeah, we had a good time, didn't we? So many close games. Those were the days. But, I have to be honest with you. I enjoy watching more than coaching."

"I agree. Besides, our boys outgrew our knowledge of the game a long time ago." Jeff paused for a second and readjusted his hat. "So, how are things? You sounded pretty frenzied when we spoke a couple of weeks ago."

Steve looked around to make sure no one heard what Jeff said. "Not much better, unfortunately. But Jennifer Silverstone came to my office today. I think I'm going to have her help me." *Now Jeff's going to know what a loser I am since I had to hire Jennifer. Great.*

Jeff's voice became warm. "Yeah, Jennifer is great. What do you think of her reporting and forecasting programs?"

"I don't know anything about them." Steve began fidgeting with his watch, rotating it back and forth on his wrist.

"Oh, well I don't want to steal her thunder or anything, but I can't tell you how much clarity she brought to me and how much that helped my company. Her scorecards and reports have shed a whole new light on my business' performance and empowered me to make better decisions." Jeff smiled somewhat sheepishly. "I saved my business and I'm back to where I

30

needed to be the whole time, running my business the way it should be run."

"Wow, that's quite an endorsement. I thought you were on top of everything and didn't need consultants." Steve felt a little less self-conscious.

Jeff laughed. "You really think that? I learned a long time ago I need to hire people who are really smart with the stuff I don't know anything about."

Emma appeared from the bathroom just as Jeff finished speaking. "Dad, can we go get the licorice now?" Emma grabbed her father's hand and began leading him to the student-run snack bar.

"Jeff, great seeing you. I wanted to talk to you about something else. Can I call you next week?" Steve asked over his shoulder.

Jeff raised his eyebrows and smiled. "Sure. I can see you have your hands full." Jeff winked at Emma and she giggled.

Steve was physically with his family the rest of the night, but his mind was somewhere else. *I'm going to ruin a lot of people's lives next week. Maybe I should just shut the entire company down. But I can't fail. My family will be so ashamed of me. I can't let them down like that.*

IMPACT INSIGHT #8
Entrepreneurs often struggle to separate business problems and family life, especially when their business is not doing well.

8
BOMB

Steve spent most of Saturday in his home office reading through email, mostly with bad news, and reviewing which of his employees would be the first to let go. *None of my staff is bad. I'm mostly cutting employees that I wouldn't hesitate to hire back if things pick up again. This would be a lot easier if I had five employees who deserved to be fired.*

Steve was uninterrupted until late in the afternoon. A quiet knock on his door was followed by a sweet, feminine voice. "Dad, I know you're busy, but can I come in? I want to ask you something."

Before he could answer, the door opened and Zoe, his 12-year-old daughter, entered. She was tall for her age and sported a headband that held back her thick, black, curly hair, as usual. Today it was pink and brown with a large flower on the side, one of Steve's favorite headbands. She looked cute and fun.

"Dad, I need your help with a school project. My teacher wants me to interview you."

Steve pushed his chair back from the desk. "Interview me? What class is this for?"

"Social studies. We're supposed to write a history of an important event in our family. I've decided to write about you and Mom getting married, since that was the start of this family."

Steve sighed. "Really? So what do you have to turn in?"

Zoe handed the assignment paper to Steve. "A five-page paper along with the notes I take from interviewing at least two eyewitnesses to the event.

I've picked you and Mom, obviously. It's due on Monday, so I need to get it done."

"Zoe, I'm really under a lot of pressure right now. Is there anyone else you can interview in my place? How about Grandpa?" Steve felt like his words sucked all of Zoe's enthusiasm for the project right out of her. She slung her head down, but clenched her fists. "Why can't you just talk to your Mom?" He added with desperation, "She planned the whole thing anyway."

Zoe's voice became more resolute. "Maybe Mom is right about you! You're just a selfish jerk!"

Steve rocked back like an offensive lineman hit by a blitzing linebacker. "Right about me? Selfish jerk? Where's this coming from?"

Zoe's face turned as pink as her headband. "You know what I'm talking about. You're the one who made Mom so sad she cried the other night!"

Steve felt like his heart had been ripped out of his chest and run over by a dump truck. "Zoe, why on earth are you saying these things?"

"Don't play dumb, Dad. I heard Mom crying on the phone the other night to Aunt Emily. She told her that you didn't seem to care about her or anyone else in the family and that you love that stupid business more than her or anyone else." Zoe's eyes remained angry but her lower lip began to wobble. "She's right. You only care about your company."

Steve couldn't feel anything except the surreal bewilderment that immediately follows a catastrophic event or natural disaster, like when he first saw the planes crash into the World Trade Center towers on 9-11.

Zoe lowered her voice. "I just wanted an interview, Dad. Now I'm going to flunk this assignment because of you. You're really messed up."

Steve started to say, "Just ask your mom," but Zoe was gone.

Steve never felt more alone. He wanted to march out of his office and yell up the stairs at Aubrye. *How dare she pull Zoe into their quarrel? Everyone and everything seems to be lining up against me.*

Steve tightened all of his upper-body and neck muscles and let out a low, forceful grunt, wishing he could be anyone else, anywhere else.

9
GUT

After a long, depressing weekend of entering numbers into a calculator as if it could magically make his business problems disappear, Steve worried Monday's meeting with Jennifer would be more of the same. He sat in the office of Bolty's corporate headquarters, not sure if Monday at the office or the weekend at home was worse.

He pulled a pad of paper from his bag. He flipped to the fifth page to review a list he made over the weekend of the barriers to getting the business back on track. At the top of the list, he'd printed: BARRIERS TO BOLTY'S RECOVERY. *Everything I've worked so hard to build is hinging on these. Seeing the six main items on this list makes saving this company even more daunting.*

Jennifer entered Steve's office, pulled off her overcoat, and hung it on the back of her chair. Steve thought about Jennifer earning an MBA, something he had wanted to do but had never had the time to make it happen. *I should have done that. Maybe if I did, I would be as calm and self-assured as she is right now.*

Jennifer extended her hand and shook Steve's. "Steve, how are you? I hope you didn't worry too much about the business over the weekend."

He barked out a laugh that sounded not only unhappy but urgent. "Well, let's say the business was just one of my worries. But I survived. How about your weekend?"

Jennifer pulled her iPad from her bag and placed it on Steve's desk as she sat down. "I couldn't help but think about Bolty, this business you've worked so hard to build. I started to put some things together that will help us figure out this layoff, but I still have some work ahead of me before I'll be ready to make any observations or recommendations."

Steve settled himself into his chair, but immediately sat forward, leaning on his desk, his nerves making it feel like the seat back was covered with hot broken glass. "Well, I hope you don't take this the wrong way, but it's a little comforting to hear that someone besides me was thinking about this company over the weekend."

IMPACT INSIGHT #9
Being an entrepreneur is often a lonely endeavor, with few or no others that care about the business as much as the owner does.

"I'm not sure if I should take that as a compliment or a reminder that I work too much." Jennifer's grin showed a little fatigue, something Steve hadn't noticed before.

Jennifer sat down in a leather chair in front of Steve's desk. Steve noticed his bookshelf, lined with business books full of interesting information but of little help to him now.

Jennifer fidgeted with her iPad, as if to make sure it was powered on. "Do you remember us talking briefly last week about the transition every business owner must make? Well, at least every business owner that wants to grow their business beyond their ability to be involved in every day-to-day detail?"

Steve thought for a moment. "Now that you mention it, yes I do."

"Good. Let me try and summarize your journey as an entrepreneur." Jennifer was startled by a loud banging in the next office. The wall muffled the noise, but it sounded like two metal pots colliding at full force.

Steve shrugged his shoulders. "Sorry about the noise. We converted the office next to mine into a testing, repair, and general utility room for the engineers. They're likely testing how some electrical components hold up under some, shall we say, pressure."

"Oh, okay." Jennifer took a deep breath and appeared to gather her thoughts. "When you first started your business, you were likely involved in every single detail of it. I'll bet you knew all of your first customers personally because you were the one that sold them. Is that right?"

"Yes, you're right." Steve tried to ignore the thumping, then relaxed a bit when it quickly subsided. "I knew most of them from the prior company where I worked."

Jennifer nodded. "And, I'll bet you knew all of your vendors and suppliers because you personally negotiated your contract and relationship with them. Is that right?"

"Right again."

Jennifer pointed to the thirty cubicles, filled with busy employees, just outside Steve's door. "And, I'll bet you knew all of your initial employees personally because you were either related to them or you had known them long before you ever started the business." She winked. "Am I three-for-three?"

"Yes, you're right on." Steve briefly reflected on the early days of the business. He remembered how nervous he was when he sold his first client, and he cringed to think about some of those early hires who he thought would work out well. What a disaster that had been. His cousin Lisa still hasn't spoken to him since her husband had been let go for poor performance years ago.

IMPACT INSIGHT #10

With a boot-strapping mentality, most start-up businesses require the founders to wear most, if not all, of the hats of responsibility.

"Funny how I thought I knew what I was doing but I really wasn't prepared to start this business." Steve looked at his hand-drawn timeline of Bolty's life. "I made a lot of mistakes back then. And, in some ways, I'm still making a lot more."

"We all are," Jennifer said. "But those early days were very critical to you developing your intuition for running your business." The loud banging began again and Jennifer paused, clearly distracted for a moment. She held up her hand, fingers extended, and ticked off the next list, finger by finger. "Your intuition is the way you assimilate the information you glean from your business to understand, one, where you've been, two, where you are now, three, where you're going, four, what's going well, and five, what needs to be improved. It's a conscious process that helps you make the best decisions you can. Many call it their 'gut.'"

"Well, I've got one of those." Steve looked down at the 30 pounds he had added to his midsection since he started the business. Running Bolty and keeping up with family and other responsibilities were not always conducive to good eating and exercise habits. He'd been in a lot better shape when he was coaching his son, he remembered with even more regret.

Jennifer grinned. "The point of this is that in the early days you collected all of your information directly from the sources, your customers, suppliers, and employees, because you were involved in every detail of the business. It was all qualitative data, and you trained yourself to process this information and make decisions based on it."

Steve started to feel a little uncomfortable with how this person he'd known for only a couple of days could describe him so accurately.

"Here's how this may have worked in the early days of your business." Jennifer pointed to the phone. "One of your first customers called you to complain that some of your work was failing. You were able to quickly and efficiently diagnose and solve the problem because you had sold the solution, done most of the programming yourself, and micro-managed anyone else or any vendors that worked on the project. Did anything like this ever happen?"

Steve was quick with his response. "Yes, it happened at least a couple of times per week for the first several years of the business."

"You were using qualitative information, a phone call from a customer and your intimate knowledge of the situation, to make decisions."

Steve pondered for a moment. "I guess you're right. And here I thought I was unique. Seems like you see stuff like this all the time."

"The interesting thing about using qualitative information is that it's

38

extremely effective while a company is still small and has a hands-on owner who's engaged in every detail." Jennifer raised her hands around a large, imaginary ball. "But eventually most businesses grow too large or have an absentee owner that makes it impossible for them to effectively function on qualitative data alone to make decisions."

> **IMPACT INSIGHT #11**
> *Being involved in every detail is cost effective for start-ups, but it teaches founders bad habits that can limit growth and opportunity.*

Steve leaned forward, trying to absorb what Jennifer was describing. "So, what do they, I mean we, do?"

"They, or we, have to transition to relying on quantitative data, information that represents the qualitative data an entrepreneur or business owner used when the business was smaller and less complex. Most entrepreneurs develop a very good intuition, or 'gut' for their business, but usually have to train themselves to process and assimilate quantitative data along with the qualitative, or what becomes anecdotal, information."

Steve wasn't buying-in immediately. "What about that customer with the problem? Are you telling me that I shouldn't listen to what my customers have to say anymore?"

"No, I'm not saying that at all. What I'm saying is that qualitative information just needs to be put in context with the quantitative data. Let's refer to the same example but add some details and context. What if you looked into the customer's problem and learned that the customer had not received what was promised because he was actually more than six months late on paying you? His project was on hold until he brought his account current. Further data showed that this customer represented less than 0.5% of your total revenue. Now we have a completely different perspective on the customer's complaint, don't we?"

"Yes, I see your point." Steve looked at his degree from Pepperdine on the wall.

"The best part about this example is that in the early days of the business, you would have known all of that information--that he was late with payment and that he was a very small customer. But as a business grows, it becomes impossible for you to know all of that information off the top of your head, so you need to rely on reports. In this case, you likely would need a weekly or monthly Accounts Receivable aging report and a customer and project concentration report, for example."

"I think I get it. But how do I know when I reach the point that I need to rely on this quantitative type of information?" The obnoxious banging next door was now a distraction to Steve, who was trying to grasp what Jennifer was teaching him.

"It depends on several factors. The complexity of the business and product or services mix is a big one, along with growth trajectory and overall size and scope of the business. It's usually never too early to start introducing the use of numbers to run the business in a company's life cycle. But with the number of employees you have I'll bet you're at a point you could get a lot of value from the use of quantitative data."

> **IMPACT INSIGHT #12**
> *Not transitioning to the use of IMPACT quantitative data will eventually hinder an organization's ability to grow and keep the entrepreneur from building the most valuable business possible.*

"Well, we seem to be okay so far." Steve was so programmed to telling everyone that the business was doing well, regardless of how it was actually doing, he momentarily forgot that Jennifer knew Bolty was struggling. He quickly restated his comment. "Or, at least we have survived to this point."

"My point is that using the right kind of quantitative information could have possibly helped you be more successful during the past several years. Without knowing too much detail about your business, I might even make the assertion that you wouldn't be in such a tough spot right now if you were using the principles I'm going to cover." Jennifer lowered her head, almost like a child who just talked back to a parent. "Is that too bold of a statement or do you think there might be some truth in it?"

Steve initially felt defensive, but tempered that to acknowledge his deficiencies in using quantitative data to run things more efficiently. "So this is going to solve all my problems? I have six main items I'm struggling with right here." Steve held up the pad on which he had written his list, feeling he should have headed the list with the words: MY FAILURES.

"Numbers and data probably won't solve problems alone, but they will empower you and your team to know how to discover, address, and resolve pertinent issues before they become major disasters. And if anything ever does become a major problem, quantitative data will help you know how to fix it. The right kind of quantitative data removes a lot of what feels like guesswork right now and replaces it with clarity. And clarity seems to always help you make improvements in your business."

IMPACT INSIGHT #13
When used correctly, quantitative data can improve performance, decision-making, acumen, and, most importantly, chances for success.

Steve was intrigued. He was also open to any suggestions that could help him run his business better. He was sick of feeling overwhelmed, overmatched, and overworked.

10
IMPACT

Steve looked at his consultant, Jennifer, who had just demonstrated she understood his challenges far better than anyone else in his life. *Those other entrepreneurial companies she worked for must have appreciated her a lot, not to mention the several clients she's currently helping.* He wished he had met her before his company was in shambles. *Even if I did know her back then, I doubt I would have believed I really needed outside help.*

"Jennifer, just before you got here I finished making a list of all of my biggest and most daunting problems. I know we're going to work on this potential layoff for the next couple of days, but there's more to fixing my business than just that. I want you to know what you're getting yourself into."

Steve stood and walked to the whiteboard next to his window. After erasing the rough diagram of a mobile device and its electrical components, he picked up the blue marker. "You'll notice that I'm going to put a small square next to each problem--so I can put a checkmark in it when we've solved each one." *Thinking I'm going to be able to check off just one of these items is probably overly optimistic.* He sighed.

Jennifer moved her iPad to her lap and began to type notes. "I'm ready."

If I'm letting her in, then she's going to get it all. Steve's palms were sweaty as he gripped the marker and wrote the entire list on the board. *I must be pretty uncomfortable writing all my failures on this board.* The banging next door had stopped, and his office was gravely quiet. The list read:

- [ ] Barely made payroll
- [ ] Out of cash
- [ ] Key employees left
- [ ] Large customer left
- [ ] IRS, Lawsuit, Vision for future
- [ ] Financial leader deficiencies

When he finished writing, Steve returned to his chair and swung it around until he faced the whiteboard, with Jennifer to his back. Steve looked at the list like a climber just starting his journey to the top of Mt. Everest.

"I know these things may appear insurmountable." Jennifer's voice sounded apologetic. "But I don't see any reason why we can't solve each one. I'm jumping a little ahead of myself, but do you mind if I write next to each of these problems the tool we're going to use to solve them?"

"Not at all. That would be great. Maybe with your help I'll be able to solve them all."

Jennifer walked to the whiteboard, picked up the red marker, and began writing. When she was done, the list looked like this:

PROBLEM	SOLUTION
Barely made payroll	Monthly IMPACT Indicators
Out of cash	Quarterly IMPACT Forecaster
Key employees left	Daily/Weekly IMPACT Indicators
Large customer left	Annual IMPACT Forecaster
IRS, Lawsuit, Vision for future	5-Year IMPACT Forecaster
Financial leader deficiencies	IMPACT CFO Services

"That reminds me. I saw Jeff last Friday night and he mentioned something about your reporting and forecasting programs. Those can really solve my problems?" Steve pointed to the solutions Jennifer had added to his list.

"Well, they bring you the quantitative data you need to successfully manage and grow your business. These reports remove guesswork and anxiety, which I know you've been experiencing and are probably sick of. Am I right?"

Steve nodded. Jennifer returned to the chair in front of Steve's L-shaped oak desk. "This will improve your decision-making process and empower you to confidently make the best decisions you can. Let me start by explaining the acronym IMPACT."

IMPACT INSIGHT #14
There is no problem in business that can't be quantified, affording the clarity needed to overcome almost any challenge entrepreneurs face.

Steve spun his chair around to face her. The two spent the next several minutes discussing what IMPACT stood for and how it applied to helping his business. Jennifer displayed a picture, each letter of IMPACT down one side and the corresponding word each letter stood for on the other.

Jennifer put the iPad down. "Let's use a real life example to help you see what I mean. Do you have a copy of your most recent set of monthly financial and operations reports?"

"Judy gave me the monthly report just last week, but I can't remember where I put it." Steve was embarrassed to admit he hadn't even looked at it, mainly because he was always confused by what Judy's report meant. He knew he should spend more time analyzing it, but even when he did, he never learned anything useful from the numbers.

Jennifer waited while Steve rummaged through his desk. Rather than sudden bursts of banging, like before, a consistent, steady tapping permeated the walls, like a small child knocking incessantly on a door until someone opens it.

Steve found a piece of paper titled "Profit & Loss" in the stack by his computer monitor. He placed it in front of Jennifer. It showed the revenue, expenses, and profit for January, yet March was almost over. It included no percentages, just numbers and totals for one month.

Jennifer picked up the paper. "Okay, do you remember what the 'I' in IMPACT stands for?"

"Yes – Insightful." Steve felt like a high school student who just aced his college entrance exam.

"That's right. So, what insights did you gain from this report? How did it help you think more strategically about your business and what you need to do to improve it?"

Steve shook his head. "The way the information is organized doesn't match the way I think about the business, how I bid projects, and how I think about the costs and revenues that come in from those projects. It's mostly confusing to me. And I can never make sense of why my net income, or net loss as this one states, is always so different from my cash in the bank. I figured they should be about the same. I guess it's not very insightful."

"You know, most business owners I meet think the same thing about the correlation between cash and net income. But there's a reason they're different, and it is usually manifest in additional reports that come with this one." Jennifer looked at Steve's desk, as if searching for more pages. "Do you ever have a balance sheet and a statement of cash flow with this monthly profit and loss?"

"No, I don't." Steve clenched his fists, suppressing the urge to scream his frustration from the top of the snow-covered mountains out his window.

"The IMPACT reporting system will get you all of this information and help you interpret and use it to gain insights into improving your business."

Jennifer coughed, then pulled a bottle of water from her bag and took a quick drink. "Now on to the next letter. 'M' stands for Meaningful. Did this report highlight the things that are the most important to your business, like your cash flow and the activities that make you profitable?"

Steve puts his hands up. "I had no idea this acronym was going to beat me up so badly. No, it's not worth much to me in that way."

"I'm not trying to point out flaws. I just thought it would be more helpful to talk about the acronym in real application, not just in theory."

"I know. Please keep going." Steve dropped one of his hands and gestured for Jennifer to continue with the other.

Jennifer took another drink from her water bottle. "Do you remember what the 'P' in IMPACT stands for?"

"Yes--Precise. Judy pays a lot of attention to the details of how to code things, so it seems like we do pretty well with that one." The tapping quieted as Steve spoke, but then the distracting banging returned. *I think I liked the tapping better.*

"I agree with your assessment of accuracy, with one small exception--revenue recognition. We'll cover this in a little bit. Let's move on to the next--'A' is for Accessible. This has reference to two things." Jennifer raised her hand in the air with her index finger extended. "First, do you and the other members of your team have physical access to this information?"

> **IMPACT INSIGHT #15**
> *Even if an entrepreneur is receiving some reports and quantitative information, they may not meet the IMPACT criteria, meaning the entrepreneur is not getting everything he should from the information.*

Jennifer raised a second finger on the same hand. "Second, is it presented in a way that makes it intellectually accessible? This means, can it be quickly digested and interpreted rather than requiring minutes or even hours of analysis before it can be understood?"

"If it can even be understood at all." Steve chuckled, wishing he could rip up his mostly useless one-page report. "I probably should share some of this information with others in the company, but I've never done that. And it would be helpful if this report included a couple of charts or graphs that summarized the information."

"Charts and graphs that are easy to read and interpret are exactly the way to achieve intellectual accessibility." Jennifer sat up like a baseball fan anxious for the 9th inning when her team is in the lead. "'C' stands for Comparative, meaning the data is put in context next to the prior months and years of the business as well as to industry and competitor benchmarks. It doesn't look like this report makes any comparisons. Do you agree?"

Steve placed his hands on the edge of his desk and pushed his comfortable executive chair back a few inches. "Yes, although of all of the criteria you've mentioned this one makes the most sense to me. I can't remember how we did the month before the one on this report, which leads to not understanding if things are improving or getting worse."

"Exactly. Now, on to the last letter, 'T'."

"I remember this one," Steve said. "It stands for Timely."

"That's right. Usually a report like this should be produced by the 10th or 15th of the following month, so about February 15th is when you should expect it. It sounds like you didn't get this until the middle or end of March. Is that right?" Jennifer folded her arms and glanced at the calendar on the wall next to the whiteboard.

Steve applied his index fingers to his temples and gently began rubbing. "Wow, this is a lot of information to process, and it's hard for me to stare so directly at so many places where I'm failing."

Jennifer pointed at the calendar on the wall. "Steve, my point is not to focus on the past, but merely to help you understand IMPACT and how, when it governs our data, it helps us to build a successful business."

IMPACT INSIGHT #16
The IMPACT principles help every business ensure its quantitative data and reports are as effective and value-added as possible.

"I know. I realize that." A clank in the next office pulled Steve from his overwhelmed feeling. "So how do these reports work?"

"Well, we need to start with the Monthly Impact Indicators so they can help us solve the first problem on our list." Jennifer pointed at 'Barely made payroll' on the whiteboard.

Steve and Jennifer spent ten more minutes together as Jennifer gave Steve a brief overview of the fifteen to twenty-page compilation of reports, data, charts, and graphs that comprise the Monthly IMPACT Indicators. They also discussed Jennifer's fees. Then Jennifer left to spend the rest of the afternoon with Judy.

Steve thought about his timeline to finalize his staffing plan. *Jennifer says this report will have a lot of the answers I need, and she promised it would be ready for my review by Wednesday afternoon. And the fees we discussed for her services were actually more reasonable than I thought they would be.*

Steve walked to the whiteboard and stared at the freshly-written list of problems and solutions. *Will I be able to check off all of these boxes before my business and family crumble?*

11
INSIGHT

The clear, blue sky and brilliant sunlight that poured into Steve's office filled him with hope, though the March weather was still cold. Jennifer was back in the office on Wednesday morning and scheduled a meeting with Steve for the late afternoon to review her work and discuss the layoff. She would be spending the day with Judy and a few other managers as well as preparing reports and analysis for her meeting with Steve.

Steve was nervous for the outcome, but ready to get his sinking ship righted. He even felt like he should have some hope turning his relationships with his family around.

He decided to give his friend, Jeff Hanks, a call and get some advice about his failing family. *But I'm ashamed to tell my old friend how bad things have gotten. Jeff seems to have the perfect family. Come on, Steve. Just swallow your pride and make the call. I better text him to see if he's available.*

Steve texted: Can u talk 4 a few minutes?

Jeff texted back: Yep. I have about 10 mins.

Steve pressed Jeff's phone number on his iPhone.

Jeff's voice boomed through the phone. "Steve, it's too bad my son's team had to hand you a loss on Friday." Never being accused of being too quiet, Jeff's laugh was also several decibels above what Steve would consider normal.

Trying to get his own voice to booming level, Steve almost shouted. "Well, I think you're on our schedule one more time this year, so maybe we can kick the miners' tail yet." Steve's back stiffened and he bit down on his pen cap, realizing his competitive spirit was alive and well.

"So, what did you want to talk about, Steve?"

"I don't mean to take too much of your time, but I need your advice on a personal matter, which since I saw you on Friday has changed significantly."

"Shoot." Jeff lowered his voice.

"Well, I'm wondering if you and your wife, Steph, have ever argued about your business. You know, how much time you spend there and whether or not you bring the stress of it home to the family."

Jeff cleared his throat. "Steve, I'll be honest with you. My tendency to be a workaholic and my obsession with my company almost caused my marriage to fail."

"Really? I never would have guessed. Things are kind of weird with Aubrye." Steve sat in silence, not sure if he wanted to continue.

"What in the world does that mean?" Jeff's voice was a little garbled, and Steve figured it was a temporary blip in his mobile phone coverage.

"Aubrye's not happy with me right now. I'm spending a lot of time trying to fix my business and I'm not getting much support from home. I suppose I don't deserve it."

"Knowing you, any support Aubrye does give you is too much." Jeff's bellowing laugh made Steve pull the phone a few inches from his ear until it softened.

"Yeah, leave it to you to kick a man while he's down." Steve tried to keep his voice light but wondered if this call had been such a great idea.

Jeff stopped laughing, his voice becoming much friendlier. "Okay, okay. So tell me what's going on."

Steve took a deep breath. "You know my business is struggling. It's become all-consuming. Every waking hour I feel sick while I try to figure out how to fix it. I've definitely neglected my family for quite some time now. I'm frustrated and I just can't shake the feeling of being a total loser."

Jeff's voice became more serious. "Steve, I'm certainly no expert in relationships, but I've been in your shoes before. And the way you're handling it isn't very healthy. No wonder you're not Aubrye's favorite person."

Steve noticed a few employees gathered around a cubicle just outside his office. They were looking at a computer, laughing. *Probably one of those silly videos people put on YouTube. The YouTube video of my life right now is so pathetic I bet most people would laugh at it, too.*

Steve took a small bit of confidence in hearing someone he respected had gone through similar challenges. He waited to hear more about how Jeff handled it.

"When my business struggled, focusing only on saving it wasn't the best thing for me to do for my business or family. In fact, with all my focus on the business, my perspective was actually hindered and I became far less effective. And Steph thought I was pushing her away, which is why my marriage almost failed."

Steve stood, tightening his grip on his cell phone like it was a lifeline and pressing it tightly to his ear so he wouldn't miss a syllable. He got up and closed the door to his office. "Jeff, my whole life, I've never been the smartest or the brightest, but you know me, I'll work my head off to get an edge. That's just how I am. When things get tough, I'll work all night if I have to. So when things at Bolty have been bad and getting worse, I'm doing the same thing--working a ton. But my wife isn't cool with this strategy, and she's sending me some very confusing mixed signals." Steve tried to chuckle, as if that would make what he said less serious, but inside, he felt even worse.

"What do you mean by mixed signals?" Jeff asked.

Steve looked at the two-year-old photo on his wall, his smiling family all wearing denim shirts and jeans, standing in front of a beautiful waterfall. "Well, we had this argument recently where she told me that I better hurry up and fix the business if I expected to save our family. So I've been trying to do that. But then she cries on the phone to her sister that I only care about the business. I'm pouring my time into my company for her and the kids with her permission, yet she feels neglected."

"Sounds like your one-track mind is your problem, Steve," Jeff said. "She told you to go and fix the business, but I don't think she meant that you should disappear from the family. When was the last time you talked to her? You know, just sit down and listen to what she says."

"I talk to her all the time." Steve raised his voice.

"Really? Do you listen to what she says, or are you thinking about your business while she's talking?"

Steve felt like an eight-year-old who got caught eating a stolen candy bar by his mother. He didn't want to answer, but he knew his silence was answer enough. *Why couldn't Jeff just tell me how Aubrye is in the wrong here? Just one more failure for my growing list.*

Jeff continued. "Steve, I've been there. We have similar personalities and approaches to business. You can't just turn off your family while you fix your company. It'll destroy what matters to you most, your relationships with your wife and kids. You called me for advice, so I'm going to give it to you. You have to figure out how to disengage from your business, no matter how bad it gets, and engage with your family--even if it's just for a short time every day."

Steve began to pace his office floor. *How could I have been such an idiot?* "Jeff, I'm so lame. I guess I got my blinders on and charged ahead, like normal, not realizing the wake I was leaving behind."

"As someone who is guilty of the same transgression, I can only hope your experience isn't as painful as mine."

Steve was unsure how to implement Jeff's advice. "So what did you do? How did you save your marriage?"

"I had to force myself to stop thinking about the business for a couple of hours every night when I was at home. No matter what was happening at work, I compelled myself to mentally forget it and immerse myself with the family--a date night with my wife or even volunteering to coach my son's basketball team. That's when I met you, about eight years ago."

Steve's eyes widened. "Are you serious? Your business and family were falling apart when we met? I had no idea."

IMPACT INSIGHT #17
Entrepreneurs often mask their business struggles well, a conditioned response for survival that can sometimes cause denial and blindness toward the problem.

"Yeah, those were some of my darkest days," Jeff admitted. "But I realized I had to make time for my wife and kids. And the irony of it all is how much better my family and company did as a result. Coaching was a great outlet to clear my head. You'd be surprised how many ideas I got for solving problems in my business while in that basketball gym."

Steve began to think about the things he enjoyed doing with his family and how balanced he felt when he spent time with them. "Jeff, I cannot thank you enough for your time and perspective. I better let you go to your next commitment."

"Steve, please let me know if I can do anything else to help. We slow learners gotta stick together. And don't give up. Aubrye probably won't trust you at first, so you need to give it some time."

"Thanks. Talk to you soon." Steve ended the call and set his phone on his desk. He walked to his window and noticed a small tulip breaking through the soil just outside. *Things are so tense at home I bet Aubrye won't react positively to me trying to engage with her and the kids. Now I appreciate the saying about how keeping trust is easier than earning it. I hope I'm not too late and my family still trusts me a little.*

Steve's clock read 3:28 PM. He turned from the window, expecting to hear Jennifer's knock on his door any second. It was time for the layoff discussion.

12
MEASUREMENTS

Steve thought about what Jeff said, about devoting more time to family. *But right now I have to focus on this company. Then I can be the husband and father my family wants me to be.*

Steve couldn't wait another two minutes for his meeting with Jennifer. Antsy with anxiety, he left his office to find her. She was in Judy's office, packing her things, probably to come and meet with him. The sick feeling he had become so accustomed to returned when he looked at the picture of Judy's family on the wall, thinking about how many families he was about to ruin.

"Jennifer, are you ready to meet?" Steve was out of breath, hoping Jennifer's work would lead to more good news, like when she helped the company make payroll.

"Yes, we're just finishing up." Jennifer gathered several loose papers. Her business suit of pastel colors didn't match the dark ensemble Steve envisioned the executioner of his employees would wear. What did he expect, he mused wryly, a black cloak with her iPad in one hand and a sickle in the other?

"OK. Please come to my office when you're ready." Steve's uneasy voice trembled slightly.

The sick feeling in his stomach intensified as he returned to his office, walking past his forty employees who depended on this company for their livelihood. *Maybe it would be better just to close the company, but then no one would have a job. I guess I have to sacrifice some for the benefit of the rest, including me and my family.*

> **IMPACT INSIGHT #18**
> *Being a business leader means needing to make difficult decisions, and then following-through with them, regardless how unpleasant they may be.*

Steve couldn't sit, so he paced in his office to burn off some nervous energy. Jennifer arrived a minute later. "I have quite a few things on my computer to show you. Should we meet in the conference room so I can project them onto the screen and we can review them together?"

Steve liked the idea. "Sure, but let me grab my folder with everything I've done to prepare for this. I'll meet you there in a minute."

When Steve arrived, Jennifer was connecting her laptop to the projector. The large rectangular room was balanced with a sturdy, professional, rectangular table centered perfectly and surrounded with black leather chairs. As he sat down, he pulled out his notes and reports and prepared for the worst.

Jennifer handed Steve a packet of fifteen papers connected by a staple in the top left corner. The front page had 'Monthly IMPACT Indicators' on the top with a list of the reports included in the packet and a section for observations and recommendations. Steve briefly flipped through the impressive package, noticing colors, comments, charts, and graphs throughout.

"That reporting package is also on the screen." Jennifer fiddled with the projector to center the picture. Steve saw the same cover page projected in a clear, crisp image, with an attractive blue and green logo. "It will be easier for us to go over this while I point things out from page to page." Jennifer held up a small laser pointer that looked like a pen.

Steve interlocked his fingers and tightly closed his hands together. "I feel like never having this meeting, but I know I can't wait anymore. I want it over with."

Jennifer finished setting up the display and looked at Steve. "The information in this report, once understood, will define where Bolty is and give us some clues about where it's headed. We need to know this information to properly address our over-staffing issue. If it's all right with you, I'm going to jump right in."

"I'm as ready as I'll ever be," Steve said, trying to convince himself. He pictured the company Christmas party just a few months earlier with all of the employees and their families. *When I think about my employees' kids, I can barely stomach what I'm about to do.*

IMPACT INSIGHT #19
Most entrepreneurs take pride in providing jobs for employees and helping the economies in which they operate, and they do not like to let them down.

As they reviewed the information in the packet, Jennifer and Steve spent the next half-hour discussing things like liquidity, cash flow, profits, and the overall health of the business. The package of reports included balance sheet comparisons, Profit & Loss comparisons, project profitability reports, and even cash flow statements. It was a lot of information to absorb, but Steve kept up and even recalled some of the things he learned in his business classes from college.

Jennifer returned to the cover page and pointed at the explanation of the IMPACT acronym. "Just so you can see how IMPACT fits into all this, let's make sure we agree these reports meet the IMPACT criteria," Jennifer suggested. "Would you say they are Insightful, Meaningful, Precise, Accessible--both physically and intellectually, Comparative, and Timely?"

"Without a doubt," Steve responded. "I really wish I had this type of information months, or even years ago."

Jennifer nodded. "We certainly had to work to make things precise. The work-in-progress element of correcting your revenue recognition was a little tricky, but I think it came together quite well. You'll see how that works a little more clearly when we work on the Weekly and Daily IMPACT Indicators."

"It was powerful for me to see our performance compared to prior months and years. That made everything more insightful." Steve pointed to the 'accessible' part of the IMPACT definition. "I now understand what you mean by intellectual accessibility. The charts and graphs drilled right into the issues, and even I could understand them." Steve chuckled, always willing to self-deprecate, hoping to lighten the mood.

IMPACT INSIGHT #20
Charts and graphs make it easy to process lots of information, quickly gaining the clarity required to improve the business.

Jennifer smiled, followed by Steve's regretful comment. "I really wish I had this type of information months or even years ago."

"Well, from my perspective it's not too late." Jennifer's voice was reassuring. "I see some promise in the business, and there seems to be plenty of work on the short-term horizon. Now we just need to figure out how to be as profitable as we can with our current and future projects."

"With these reports and your analysis and explanation, I feel much more comfortable talking about the layoff now. I still don't like that it has to be done, though."

Jennifer set the laser pointer on the conference table and walked to the clean whiteboard next to the screen. "I have a few options and suggestions for right-sizing, but first we need to highlight three numbers from the Monthly IMPACT Indicators to carry into our discussion."

She found a blue marker and turned toward Steve. "First, we need to understand what our gross margin is and what we expect and need it to be in the future. What do we know about our gross margin?"

Steve turned to page 5 and found the following chart. Steve studied the chart for a few seconds, then began to explain it. "We talked about how the gross margin is what is left of the money we bring in after the costs associated with fulfilling the projects. And those costs are almost 100% labor--the managers, engineers, and programmers--that are directly working on projects."

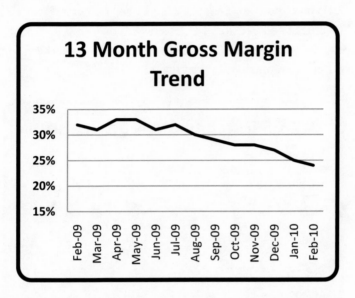

"Exactly." Jennifer smiled, making Steve feel like he was part of a winning team for a change.

In the next moment, however, he became concerned. "But our gross margin is decreasing. It should remain pretty stable, right?"

"Yes." Jennifer held up two fingers. "And two things will make our gross margin drop--a decrease in the prices we charge our customers or an increase in our costs to complete the projects, or a combination of both."

Steve sat up. "I don't think it can be our prices dropping. We've actually increased our prices over the last twelve months, thanks to an increasing level of complexity in our industry. Our competitors all did the same thing."

"Everything I've seen tells me we raised them enough to maintain a 30 - 33% gross margin." Jennifer flipped through some of her papers, then looked back at Steve. "And the industry average seems to be about 30%. We've trended to below 25% last month, which may not seem like much but has a huge impact on profit and cash flow. This is at least part of the reason we almost didn't make payroll."

Steve rested his arms on the conference table and tilted his head back. "Well, our pricing seems okay. So labor really is our problem. I can see how this percentage will be very important in determining how much labor to cut. So, that's one of the numbers. Don't we need two more?"

"Overhead and backlog. Let's start with overhead."

Steve turned to page 7 of the report to find the overhead trends chart for the last thirteen months. It looked like this:

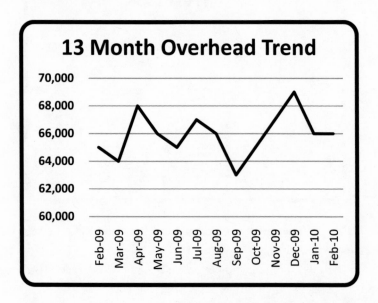

"Overhead is primarily the fixed expenses of my business, meaning they don't fluctuate much from month-to-month, even if the work we are doing on our projects increases or decreases dramatically." Steve pointed to the chart. "Looks like our overhead expenses range from about $63,000 to $69,000 per month."

Jennifer nodded. "Yes, and it averages out to be about $66,000 monthly. That's the number we need, unless you think we can cut any additional expenses from our current overhead spending."

Steve shook his head. "We're running lean and mean – we've been cutting back on everything we possibly can."

"The last number we need is our backlog. You can find the chart for it on page 9."

Steve turned the page to find the following chart, then said, "The growth in backlog during the last several months is one of the reasons I feel pretty good about Bolty's future." Jennifer's confidence in the company's future was a powerful endorsement to Steve. His trust of opinion had grown to the point that if she said the business wasn't worth keeping, he would probably shut it down. "The amount of work in front of us is growing, and it's profitable work if we can right-size our payroll."

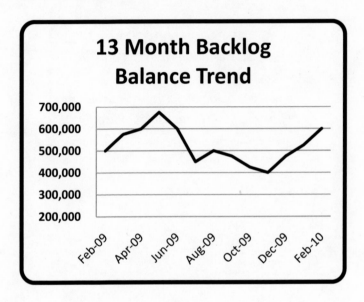

Jennifer completed her list on the board. It read:

Gross Margin: 30%
Overhead: $66,000
Backlog: $600k

Steve searched through the papers he brought to the conference room. "I tried to calculate our backlog, but your way is much more accurate. If we know this it'll help us plan how much labor we need to complete our current and future projects, right?"

"Yes, but to some extent we also need to have a feel for the market and what's going to happen beyond the work we know we already have. Jennifer replaced the cap and put the pen on the edge of the board. "But our contracted backlog gives us a solid foundation."

With the critical pieces of the puzzle on the board, Steve was ready to move into the staffing plan conversation. *With backlog going up, maybe we won't have to lay off as many people as I thought. Or maybe it will be worse.*

IMPACT INSIGHT #21

For a service business, gross margin, overhead, and backlog are very important numbers for making decisions with any type of financial ramifications.

13

REDUCTION

Jennifer walked from the whiteboard to the conference room table, removing her light-colored suit jacket and placing it over the back of her chair. Steve studied Jennifer's numbers reports. "This information, and your overall perspective, is refreshing." He wasn't looking forward to a layoff, but at least now he understood the key issues. Instead of Bolty being an albatross around his neck, he viewed his company as a wounded bird that just needed some fixing and time to heal before it could fly again.

As Jennifer sat down, Steve searched through the papers he brought with him. "Here is my list of who I think we should let go."

Jennifer rocked back in her chair, maintaining her calm and composed posture. "We need to finish our analysis before we get into names. It will help if we know exactly how much payroll we need to cut before we get into that level of detail. I saved this last part so we come to our conclusions together."

"I don't want to have to fire any employees, and it's been a stressful few days thinking about who it should be." Steve stood and began to pace at the far end of the conference room, wishing he had stayed home or maybe even gone skiing at the resort up the canyon of his favorite mountain range, the one he looked to from his window every day for strength and comfort. After all, he hadn't even gone once all season, and it was about to end.

Jennifer pulled her brown hair back, tucking it over her ears as it fell to a perfect shoulder-length. "So our next step is to figure out our break-even in terms of monthly revenue. How much project work do we need to do in a month to make payroll and cover all of our overhead expenses?"

Steve returned to his chair. "I think we need to be at about $200,000 per month. That's my best guess."

"Well, here's how I know what it is." Jennifer stood and walked to the whiteboard. "This won't be exact to the penny, but it will be very close."

Jennifer wrote the following as she calculated each number:

Overhead	$ 66,000
Divided by Cons. Gross Margin	30%
Monthly Break-Even Volume	$220,000

Jennifer underlined the bottom number. "According to this, we need to do about $220,000."

Steve wrote that number on his pad of paper and winced. "That's a little more than I thought."

"Let's keep going to see where our payroll costs need to be if we want to stop losing money." Jennifer wrote more on the board as the scent of the marker's ink carried to Steve.

Overhead	$ 66,000
Divided by Cons. Gross Margin	30%
Monthly Break-Even Volume	$220,000
Actual Payroll Costs Last Month	$193,200
$$ for Payroll at Break-Even	$154,000
Deficit Payroll Spend to Break-Even	($39,200)

IMPACT INSIGHT #22

Break-Even, in dollars, is calculated by dividing the contribution margin (which is often the gross margin in service businesses) into the fixed costs. You can convert this to units by dividing the result by the average sales price per unit.

Jennifer stepped back from the board. Pushing buttons on her calculator, she did one more calculation, then looked at Steve. "Payroll is a little more than $190,000. If we cut it by 20%, or about $40,000, and we can hit this volume of $220,000 each month, we'll stop losing money like we have for the last several months."

Steve pressed his hands against the solid oak table. "Oh no, 20% is a lot."

"I agree, but now we need to look at our backlog and future work." Jennifer dropped her calculator and it fell to the floor, similar to how Steve felt about letting some employees go--just dropping them by surprise, and leaving them to fend for themselves. Jennifer picked it up and tested a few of the keys. "Still works. Now, I think you're the best person to help with this next part. If we make a simple calculation with our break-even volume, then we can tell how many more months of work we have just to be at a break-even."

Taller than most women Steve knew, Jennifer comfortably reached the top of the whiteboard. "By the way, break-even should never be our goal. Every business exists to make a profit. Otherwise it wouldn't be worth it to the shareholder, you, to have everything at risk."

Jennifer wrote the following on the board:

Total Backlog:	$600,000
Divided by B/E Backlog:	$220,000
Months Break-Even Work:	2.7

Jennifer turned toward Steve, extending her hand under '2.7'. "If we get no more work, this is how long your company will survive if we immediately make this 20% reduction in payroll."

Steve shook his head. "That's depressing."

"Sure it is, but it's a better backlog than we have had in nine months. So our workload is improving." Jennifer handed Steve the list of the projects. "How much longer will it take to complete each of these projects?"

Jennifer returned to her seat while Steve took thirty seconds to review the list and wrote notes next to each one while referencing a few of the documents he brought. "Each of these will be done in the next three months with one exception, a small project that will take the next six months to complete.'

"OK, now I need you to pull out your crystal ball and tell me how much work we're going to get in the next few months." Jennifer smiled.

"How am I supposed to predict that?"

Jennifer crossed her legs, getting comfortable in her seat. *She must be done with the whiteboard for now.* "Well, since you see every bid, what's your feeling on the amount of work we're bidding and being awarded? Is it up, down, even?"

Steve went through a few more documents in his folder. He spoke with more confidence than he felt. "You know, things have really picked up the last few months. My feeling is that we're going to be busier."

"Okay, so I think it's fair to say that we won't do less than $220,000 in revenue in the next several months. Would you agree?"

"That sounds about right." Steve rubbed his eyes, blinked several times, then focused back on his mid-forties financial advisor.

"And do you feel confident we'll still be able to get at least the 30% gross margins on the future work?"

Steve nodded. "Yes, the pricing seems pretty consistent among our competitors. But this payroll cut is necessary to hit that, or even better margins."

Jennifer clicked several times on her laptop's mouse, retrieving another chart titled 'Break-even and Maximum Capacity'." She rested her arm on the table. "Then we need to build our staffing plan around breaking even at $220,000 of revenue per month."

Break Even

300,000	───────────
250,000	───────────
200,000	─ ─ ─ ─ ─ ─
150,000	───────────
─── Max Capacity	─ ─ Break Even

After glancing at the chart displayed on the screen, Jennifer pointed the red laser to the black line. "Our capacity, or the most work we can handle at that staffing level, is about $275,000 of work in a month. We need to operate between these two lines, break-even and maximum capacity. The closer we get to operating at our maximum capacity, we won't need to hire any more people and we'll be exponentially more profitable."

IMPACT INSIGHT #23
Maximum profit per dollar of revenue will be attained when a company operates right at its capacity.

Although the room was silent, Steve's mind was full of noise, processing what seemed like an endless amount of information from Jennifer. Steve refocused on Jennifer. "So, we need to drop payroll by about $40,000. How are we going to do that?"

"I think we basically have three options." Jennifer walked back to the board, this time picking up a red marker. She wrote:

1. Reduce everyone's pay 20%
2. Fire enough employees to reduce 20%
3. Combination of 1 and 2

The tension returned to Steve's shoulders. "What do other companies in my situation do?"

"In most cases, 20% is a lot to cut someone's pay, especially employees who live paycheck-to-paycheck. And I would imagine most of your employees fit into that category because most people generally do. Most employees can handle a 10% reduction, although that is still pretty tough." Jennifer circled number three. "In your situation, most companies do some of both to come up with the reductions they need. Those still employed after the layoff are grateful to have jobs, although you need to show them the company is on a path to return them to their original wages."

Steve pushed a piece of paper, the one with the employees listed in order of who he thought should be let go first, toward Jennifer. "I can't expect others to make a sacrifice I'm not willing to match or beat. My first suggestion is to reduce my salary 20%, a savings of more than $2,000 per month."

Jennifer sat down, marked this in her spreadsheet, and they spent the next 20 minutes trying different scenarios to reach the goal of a $40,000 reduction in monthly payroll costs.

Steve summarized the layoff plan. "We're going to let five engineers and programmers go, move one manager back into an engineer role where he will be happier anyway, and ask the remaining 35 employees to take a 10% temporary reduction in salary. And I will take a 20% reduction to my salary as well."

Jennifer looked at the clock. "It's after 5:00 PM now, so the best time to do all of this will be first thing in the morning. Then, a meeting with all of the remaining employees is usually the best way to tell them who was let go and why. This will set the stage for you to explain the sacrifices each remaining employee will need to make, temporarily, to help the company correct its course."

IMPACT INSIGHT #24
After a layoff, the remaining employees need to see the firm has a solid plan for the future or they will leave, especially the top performers.

"Oh, this stinks. There's nothing fun about ruining peoples' lives, especially when they've been good employees. But what has to be done must be done. I need to prepare some thoughts for that meeting, and I also think we should do something to help the terminated employees land on their feet. Is a few weeks of severance too generous?"

Jennifer powered down her laptop and the projector. "No, probably not. Cash is tight, but it's a one-time expense that we'll quickly recoup. Steve, you need to do what you feel is right and fair, because you're the one who has to live with it. Writing letters of recommendation and doing other things to help them find work elsewhere is also a gesture a lot of companies make."

"Well, I have some work to get ready for tomorrow." Steve walked to the whiteboard to erase the notes, not wanting anyone to know about this before he announced it the next day. "Jennifer, will you be here to help? You've become a part of my team, and everyone likes and trusts you. They'll feel better about this plan knowing that you helped create it."

"Yes, I'll be here."

Steve stood and gathered his things. "Great. I'm going back to my office. I'll probably send you an email with some more instructions for rolling out this plan. See you tomorrow."

Steve felt lighter and more confident than he had in a long time, more like the man he used to be. Sure, the news was bad and delivering it was going to be painful, but the reports and information Jennifer helped him understand were a powerful drug of clarity and insight. *Wow, being able to see and understand my business with numbers is amazing, definitely more helpful than I thought. I can get used to this.*

14
FALL

Steve spent the next couple of hours preparing for the dreaded day of payroll reductions. Letting five people go, demoting a manager, and asking everyone else to take a 10% pay cut was not going to be his easiest or most glorious moment. But he felt a renewed confidence and energy from the clarity Jennifer was helping him attain, and he was finally doing something that would help get the business straightened out.

The digital clock display in his car read 7:07 PM as he turned over the ignition and pulled out of the office parking lot. The night was cold, even though the day had been a little warmer.

His thoughts turned to his conversation with Jeff earlier in the day. *I know I need to build trust with Aubrye, but with all the medical bills from Tyler's mountain biking accident six months ago starting to stack up, I'm not sure how she's going to respond when I tell her I volunteered to take a 20% pay cut. Maybe I just won't tell her.*

The dark night pressed on Steve like an unrelenting neighbor kid who won't leave until he sells whatever fundraising stuff happens to be in season. But he was determined to not give in. Jeff said I need to forget about the business. *I've got to give it a try.*

As the garage door closed behind his car, the overhead light did not illuminate. He fumbled in the dark, feeling his way to the door. Rather than feel frustrated that no one else bothered to fix it, Steve thought back to Jeff's comments about engaging at home. This will be a great way to show Aubrye I'm not just thinking about the business.

Steve entered the bright kitchen, squinting from the drastic lighting change. Aubrye and the three girls were sitting at the table, working on some kind of art project. Steve could hear a basketball game in the family room and assumed Tyler must be watching.

At the first sight of Dad, Emma, the happy seven-year-old who always had her mind on princesses and ponies, rushed over and hugged his leg. No one else seemed nearly as happy to see him.

"Did you notice the light was out in the garage?" Steve directed his question to Aubrye.

"No, it must have just gone out." Aubrye was diligently cutting out some paper flowers.

"Well, I think I'll fix it before I grab some dinner." Steve set his bag and keys on the table, then turned and walked back to the garage.

He pictured in his mind his wife and daughters giving him a standing ovation and Tyler breaking away from the game long enough to give his dad a high five for being such an all-American good guy. *That's how they should have reacted instead of not even acknowledging my effort,* he thought as he groped through the toolbox in the dark garage to find a flashlight.

IMPACT INSIGHT #25
Building or re-establishing trust is not a one-time event. It is earned over time.

With a flashlight in his mouth and the replacement bulb in his pocket, he carefully set up a ladder in between the two cars in the high-ceilinged garage. He climbed the ladder and leaned over Aubrye's car, balancing himself with his left hand against the garage door opener. While removing the cover to reveal the burnt-out bulb, Steve's left hand slipped, causing him to become off-balance on the third step from the top of the ladder, and he began to fall. Instinctively he turned his body just in time for his back to land squarely on the hood of Aubrye's car.

It must have made quite a noise, because Aubrye and the kids seemed to immediately open the door to the garage where Steve lay. He wasn't sure if his pride or his back hurt more.

Steve dropped his flashlight during the fall and he had no idea where it went. He heard Aubrye's voice. "What happened? Where are you?"

"I'm over here." Steve groaned, then flinched when a bright light shined directly into his eyes. *Aubrye must have found the flashlight.* Steve rolled off the hood and onto his feet, still bent over. He straightened slowly, hoping to minimize the pain. *Much less than I expected.*

Instead of using the flashlight to examine the well-being of her injured husband, Aubrye was pointing the beam of light at her car, her mouth wide open. The kids pointed, and Tyler was laughing.

Aubrye finally directed the light at Steve. "Are you all right?"

"I think so. But your hood sure makes for a lousy landing spot." Steve chuckled weakly. Zoe rubbed her hand along the crunched metal oblong bowl Steve's body had formed.

"You make a lousy hood ornament," Tyler blurted, laughing even louder as he left the garage to return to the game.

Everyone went back in the house, but Steve remained to finish the job. The light bulb in his pocket somehow survived the fall. This time, however, Steve backed Aubrye's car into the driveway.

With a functional garage light on his husband-of-the-year resume, Steve proudly, but gingerly, entered the house. Aubrye looked up at Steve, her long dark hair covering part of her face. "So, that's going to be pretty expensive to fix, don't you think?"

"Yeah, I'm sure it will be. Maybe our auto insurance will cover it." Steve hoped his fall wouldn't create another bill he couldn't pay.

Steve motioned for Aubrye to follow him into his office. He picked up his bag and keys from the kitchen table and walked into the dark cave-like room. He flipped the light switch on, but it didn't help much. *What is it with the lights in this house?* He slowly lowered himself into the chair behind his desk, afraid to test the flexibility of his injured back.

Aubrye followed and stood in the doorway. He cleared his throat, then spoke in a quiet voice. "I need to tell you about what's happening at work tomorrow. I didn't want it to worry the kids, so I'd rather they not hear."

Aubrye stepped just inside the doorway and lightly closed the door. She folded her arms over her blue sweatshirt.

Steve pulled the folder from his bag that had all of his layoff notes and spreadsheets in it as well as the report Jennifer had given him earlier that day. He held it up, then set it on the desk. "I'm letting five people go tomorrow and asking everyone else to take a 10% pay cut to try and turn the company around."

Jennifer unfolded her arms and placed her hands on her hips. "Who are you firing? You can't fire Joe--he and Sara are having a baby next month."

Steve began to feel angry and defensive. He hoped his wife would be supportive, but she was already choosing sides. He pushed those feelings to the side to give her the worst news of all. "And you need to know that I'm taking a 20% cut. I think the employees need to see that I'm willing to sacrifice if I'm asking them to give something up. It probably won't be very pretty."

Aubrye dropped her arms and tightened her fists. "You're reducing your pay by how much? How are we supposed to survive on that and pay all of Tyler's medical bills? And a new hood." She clearly intended the sting Steve felt.

"The company is on the brink of not making it. I have to do this or else very few of the good employees will want to stay. Without them, we might as well shut the company down, meaning we take a 100% pay cut."

IMPACT INSIGHT #26
Sacrifice is inherent with entrepreneurship, as business owners are usually the first to give something up for the betterment or even the survival of the company.

Aubrye put her hands back on her hips. "I'm not sure you really understand how much it costs to run this house. This is going to make things very tight. We haven't paid any of the bills from Tyler's biking accident. I don't see how we'll have a single cent left to start paying those off. The last thing I want to do is go back to work, but I will if I have to."

"Well, I don't think this puts anyone in a very good position. And I think you being home with the kids has been a huge blessing in their lives. I don't want to change that unless we absolutely have to." Steve purposefully softened his tone. "I'm sorry about your car, and I'm sorry about this pay cut. I'm sorry about Tyler's accident, but at least we don't have to worry like we did when he was first hurt."

"Yeah, it was touch-and-go there right after the accident. I just hope Bolty can squeeze out a little profit for us this year, or we may not be able to make it." Aubrye left the office and resumed her position as art director at the kitchen table. Steve followed her, taking each step gingerly, afraid any sudden movement would shoot pain through his whole body. *I'm not sure Bolty's going to survive, let alone make a profit this year.*

Knowing he was not her favorite person at that moment and hadn't been for some time, Steve decided to warm up to Tyler and catch some of the game. Steve grabbed an open bag of potato chips from the kitchen counter. He stuffed a few into his mouth, dropping a few crumbs on his way to the family room. Aubrye glared at him, so he quickly bent over and tried to pick them up. He thought his back might crack in half, but he got most of the crumbs.

"So, who's winning the game?" Steve plopped down into the couch next to Tyler.

Tyler kept his eyes on the TV. "Do you even know who's playing, Dad?"

"I have no idea," Steve admitted. "But I thought we could maybe spend a little time together watching the game."

"This game's a blowout. I gotta finish up some homework before bed." Tyler tossed the remote to Steve as he popped up from the couch and headed to his room upstairs, leaving Steve alone.

One chip at a time, Steve ate the entire bag. When the game ended, Steve felt sick, his back ached, and he realized 'engaging' with his family was going to be harder than he thought.

15
ROLLOUT

Steve's alarm clock buzzed, blaring 5:45 AM in bright red at him. Stiff and sore from landing on the hood of his wife's SUV the night before and still a little sick to his stomach from the potato chip feast, he turned off the alarm and crept to the bathroom, hoping to not wake Aubrye or anyone else in the family.

As he showered and dressed for the day, he pictured in his mind the upcoming conversations with his soon-to-be-terminated employees. *There's just no way to sugarcoat it.* He pulled the knot a little too tight on his tie, then loosened it a bit. *I just need to be honest and thank them for their loyal service.*

As usual, he made one last stop at the mirror before leaving. He couldn't help but notice a few more gray hairs calling attention to themselves against his thinning black hair. *One for each employee I'm letting go.*

Aubrye's hood looked even worse this morning, as if it continued to collapse and take on an even more grotesque form during the night. Maybe he just hadn't noticed how bad it really was, considering the trauma and mockery he experienced during the events of the night before.

He pulled out of the garage to a dark sky starting to yield to a sunrise maybe another thirty minutes away. *This is certainly a new day in the history of Bolty. Getting the employees to take a 10% pay cut will be tough. I wonder if some will leave. I imagine some will put their resumes out to see if they can find something better. I would*, he realized. *Word of this is going to get to my competitors, and they'll certainly have a field day with it.*

He leaned forward in the driver's seat, struggling to find a comfortable position for his bruised back. Like a wounded soldier going into a dog fight, he needed to forget the pain and complete the mission in front of him. *I wish I could visit that really good chiropractor downtown, but I don't have the money for it now.*

The first to arrive at the office by at least an hour, he unlocked the large glass door and unarmed the security system. He loved the quiet, dark office in the morning and allowed himself a few minutes of peace, forcing himself to not worry about the coming day's trauma and drama. Unable to impede his anxiety, however, he mentally crossed his fingers and hoped the changes to payroll would keep his business alive.

As the employees slowly started to arrive, Steve put the finishing touches on his notes for the speech he was going to give to the staff later that morning. Planning to begin at 8:15 AM with the first of five employees to let go, Steve looked at his clock--7:55 AM.

Steve walked to Judy's office and shut the door. He remembered her reaction when he told her the night before what would transpire this morning. Pretending to be in front of a large audience, Steve cleared his throat and placed his right hand over his right eyebrow in a military-style salute. He raised his voice a little louder with each word. "Private Steve Loveland, reporting for 'take jobs and money away from everyone' duty."

Steve dropped his hand to his side. "After that, put me in front of the firing squad. It'd be a blessing, I think."

Judy rolled her eyes. "Oh, I'll just be glad when this is over. When do you want me to gather everyone for the meeting again?"

Steve looked like the captain of a football team, trying to motivate his team to somehow think they could survive, or maybe even beat, the opponent, who was twice his group's size, strength, and skill. "I should be ready for the meeting at 9 AM. But I'm meeting with Phil last to explain his demotion from manager back to being an engineer. Please wait until I call him into my office, then let everyone know we'll meet in the conference room 15 minutes after that."

Steve was about to start into a pep talk, but Judy interrupted him. "Steve, I've worked with you a long time. I've seen you make a lot of decisions, and you have always been honest and fair. I just want you to know that I think you are doing the right thing. You've got my support, although

80

the pay cut is going to hurt a little."

"Thanks, Judy. We're going to make it through this. We have to. Do you have the final paychecks ready?" Judy handed him the five envelopes on the corner of her desk. Steve opened the door and walked toward his office.

Jennifer arrived, carrying a stack of papers, and she went straight to the conference room. Steve had sent an email to her the night before with the details of how he wanted the events of the day to transpire. *Good, she remembered to print the charts so she can review them with the employees.*

Steve walked into his office and set the envelopes on his desk. *I hope my plan for today goes well. I can't wait any longer. I'm ready to get this over with.*

He turned around and headed toward Joe's cubicle. Joe had been with the company a little over two years, and his wife, Sara and Steve's wife, Aubrye had built a friendship at a few company parties. They had even arranged a couple of play dates for the kids. *Aubrye is not going to be happy about this.*

"Joe, would you please come chat with me in my office?"

Joe nodded and followed Steve. Steve considered all of the reasons Joe's name was on the layoff list. He hadn't really integrated with the company's main programming language. His managers always said positive things about his personality but were always concerned about his performance. He just wasn't getting it, and it was clear he wasn't going to. He was one of the company's last hires before the economy, and the company, started to deteriorate.

"Have a seat." Steve pointed to the chairs in front of his desk. Joe sat on the edge of the chair closest to the door. His blue eyes became wary and Steve wondered if Joe knew what was coming. Uncharacteristically, Steve sat in the chair next to him rather than across the desk. Before he spoke, Steve remembered some advice he had heard years earlier. When you fire someone, don't give a long list of reasons or try to make them feel good about it. Be direct and just let them go. Otherwise, it will turn into a debate.

"Joe, I owe it to you to be straight and direct with you. We have to make some changes in this company. Our work level has dropped, and I'm afraid I'm going to have to let you go. I realize this may not seem like the best timing for you, but it's unfortunately what we have to do." Steve paused, waiting to see Joe's reaction.

Joe didn't speak, and his facial expression didn't even change.

Steve found his direct speech was coming easier. "I want to help you land on your feet as best as I can, so I'll pay you for the rest of this week and for the following two weeks as well."

Steve reached for the stack of five envelopes, found Joe's on the top, and extended it to him. "I'm also preparing a letter of recommendation for you and will email it as well as send you a hard copy in the next couple of days. I'm happy to be a reference in your search for new employment." Joe took the envelope. *It's not much, but it's probably more than I should have done considering Bolty's sick financial state.*

Steve had been through layoffs before, with Intergratech Manufacturing once and then with IPS when he shut that company down before starting Bolty, and he knew employees could be very irrational right after they learn of their termination. He carefully planned how he would handle each employee to minimize drama and backlash, mainly concerned about its effect on the remaining employees while remaining compliant with strict laws dealing with this exact situation. "In order to make this simple and dignified, we will exit my office together and I will walk with you to your desk. You can take a minute to gather your things, then I'll need to escort you to the front door. We're having a company meeting in about an hour, so everybody will know what has happened then. Please don't reach out to anyone until this afternoon. And if you do, I'm asking you to please be respectful and professional. It will just be better for everyone that way."

Joe looked like a child who just had his Halloween candy stolen. "Steve, I don't understand. I want to work here. I really need this job."

"I'm sorry, Joe. But this is something I have to do for the company. I'll do whatever I can to help you find another job."

"So, that's it. This is all I get for working harder for you than anyone else I've ever worked for." Joe's voice became louder as he sat up. "I really thought I had a future here. Sara is going to be so upset. Why me? Why not someone else?"

"Joe, not that this will make you or me feel any better, but there are others who are being let go this morning, as well."

This was the point where Steve knew he needed to bring the conversation to an end or else Joe would probably be in his office all morning. "So I can walk you out now, and then Judy will forward the letter of recommendation as soon as I complete it along with some other resources to help you in your new search. She will also be available to answer any questions about benefits. It really has been a pleasure getting to know you, and I only hope for your success."

Steve stood and walked to his office door. He waited for Joe to stand, then he opened the door and the two walked to Joe's desk. After two minutes, the two were in the reception area and Steve spoke. "Thank you for your service, Joe. I wish you all the best."

The two shook hands, neither one too enthusiastic. Joe exited the building and walked slowly to his car in the parking lot. Steve turned and headed toward his next victim, dreading the fact that he would have to do this four more times.

Steve followed the same pattern with the other employees, and then Phil. Each had a slightly different but predictable response to the news. No tears, thank goodness, but it was one of the most unpleasant mornings of his life. Phil seemed relieved with his demotion, admitting he was a bit overmatched as a manager and much more comfortable moving back to his previous role as an engineer.

When Steve entered the conference room full of 35 employees and Jennifer who were mostly standing, a few seated at the table, the room became silent, like when the school principal walks into a rowdy classroom. He made his way toward Judy and Jennifer at the front. *Word must have already spread. Do they think I'm public enemy number one?*

Steve broke the palpable tension in the room. "So, I'm guessing you all know why we're here."A nervous laugh gently erupted and then quickly died.

"Let me take a minute to tell you what's been happening for the last couple of years at Bolty. Many of you were here when the economy was booming and we were growing quickly. Those were very successful times for us. But as things have slowed down, we haven't laid anybody off. We also haven't replaced anyone who's left. Well, the truth is that our volume of work slowed faster than employees left, meaning we have been over-staffed for quite some time."

Steve looked around the room. "I have a question for those of you who've been with Bolty for more than three years. Do any of you feel as busy today as you were three years ago? Go ahead and raise your hand if you do."

No hands went up. Steve wanted to fast forward time so this upsetting meeting would be over. He placed his hands on the conference table and leaned forward. "I was hoping we could avoid a layoff and that some of the volume of work would come back, but it just hasn't. And I don't think it has anything to do with a lack of effort on anybody's part."

Steve gestured at Jennifer. "Jennifer has helped me see that we've been losing money, hand-over-fist, for the last while. We've depleted a lot of the profits from the past and we're basically out of money to be able to sustain any more losses moving forward. Now we have some good work in progress, and the market for our services continues to look promising, but we have to 'right-size' our payroll to the amount of work we're currently doing and we think we will get in the foreseeable future."

Steve held up his left-hand and separated the fingers as far apart from each other as he could. "I let five people go this morning as well as asked Phil to step down as a manager and move back into an engineer role where he's been so effective for us for so many years." Steve briefly named the five terminated employees, with gasps and sighs between each name.

"These are good people, and we sincerely hope the best for them. Bolty will do everything it can to help them land on their feet. But they aren't the only people I'm asking to make sacrifices for the sake of the company. You see, even after laying off your coworkers our payroll is still too high. But rather than lay anyone else off, I wanted to try and keep as many of you employed as I could."

Steve took a minute to try and make eye contact with each of the 35 employees in the anxiety-filled room. "Effective immediately, I'm reducing my salary by 20%. And I'm asking all of you to reduce your pay by 10% until we can get this company completely back on track. We have three solid months of work in our backlog, and we're bidding more work now than we have in a long time. You are all great employees, and I believe we're going to have enough work to keep everyone employed here. We need to grow the amount of work we do over the next six to twelve months to get your pay raised back to where it was, and I think we can do it. But it means I'm asking each of you to shoulder some of the burden, and I don't take that lightly."

A few employees dropped their heads and did not make eye contact with Steve the rest of the meeting. Others murmured quietly to their

84

neighbor. One man, Jim, who had been a programmer for about three years, was a pit-bull, about to lunge on a smaller creature.

"I need to be clear about one more thing. When Jennifer and I went over the numbers, I confirmed and reconfirmed that this layoff and wage reduction plan was deep enough to have the impact we need it to. I don't want to have to go through this again. If our volume drops significantly we will likely have to do this again, but that doesn't seem possible in the near future."

Steve walked to the back of the room, weaving between people. Everyone's eyes followed him except those who would not look up. "Some of you may not like this. In fact, all of you may not. If you can't live with it, then please feel free to step forward in the next 24 hours so that we can reduce the financial impact this will have on everyone else who chooses to stay."

Jennifer smiled and nodded her head. Steve had never mentioned this to her, but he was glad to see her approval.

Steve returned to the front of the rectangular conference room. "I need to finish with one last thing. The more I've thought about these changes, the more excited I am about our future. With some of the new, more complex projects we're taking on and the increased demand for our competencies, I think Bolty is positioned to be very competitive and successful in the future."

Steve placed his left hand on the back of the chair in which one of his employees sat. "We're going to become an organization with more clarity and direction, and Jennifer is going to help us drill that down to how each of you can help us progress every day you come to work. I hope you choose to continue to be a part of this team."

Steve moved toward the door. "I need to go and meet with one of our customers at their facility to discuss taking on a few more of their projects. But Judy and Jennifer will go over the details of how this is going to work. I'll be in my office this afternoon after 2 PM, and I've purposely cleared my schedule so that any of you may come and ask me questions or discuss any concerns you have."

Steve left the room and went to the reception area. He checked the parking lot for a band of disgruntled, recently terminated employees and their families waiting to yell at him, or maybe do something even worse. But there wasn't a soul in sight. He exhaled as he exited the building and then breathed in the fresh, cool air outside. Steve had set up this customer visit the night before as part of his plan to allow the employees to speak openly and honestly with Judy, Jennifer, and each other after he announced the layoff and 10% reduction. He wasn't sure what he'd find when he returned, but he knew the mourning and healing process would begin and hopefully end more quickly with him out of the office for a few hours.

I know one thing for sure. Not very much actual work is going to get done today. But we'll quickly move to bigger and better things tomorrow. I hope.

16
AFTERMATH

Steve returned to the office at 12:30 PM. The parking lot was about as full as it normally was, so at least he hadn't caused a mass exodus from his company yet. He had worried that the only cars left would be his, Judy's, and Jennifer's.

He pulled out his mobile phone and sent Judy the following text: r u in ur office?

While he waited for her reply, he questioned if he had handled this the right way. Jennifer was supportive of it, but Judy had had some doubts. *That's why I left. I guess I'm going to find out pretty quickly how it all went while I was gone.*

Judy texted back: yes

Steve entered the building and went straight for her door. He thought the employees would be standing around wasting the day away, talking about the events of the morning. He was surprised to see people sitting at their cubicles working, or at least it looked like they were working. He waited for black looks from a few people, especially Jim, but thankfully, several people smiled warily and everyone else kept their eyes down.

Sam Davenport, a tall, skinny man with dark hair and a shaggy beard who had worked for Steve for more than 10 years, stopped him before he got to Judy. "How did the meeting with the customer go?" Curiosity combined with anxiety filled his rather tinny voice. "Are they going to give us more work?"

Sam was a programming genius, and he had developed into a good team manager as well. He had earned the respect of everyone at the company, but Steve had to stay after him to keep his beard neatly trimmed, especially when customers were coming to visit. In all the years Steve had known him, Sam had never once asked about prospective work.

"Actually, it went quite well." Steve leaned against the short wall of the nearest cubicle. "They didn't make any firm commitments, but I think we've got a very good shot. They'll be making a decision by the end of next week."

Sam stroked his straggly beard, seemingly worried, but then smiled. "That's good news, Boss. We're all keeping our fingers crossed that good old Bolty can come back fighting. I need my job, and getting my old salary back would be pretty nice, too."

Sam turned and walked down the hall. Not sure what to think of it, Steve found Judy and closed her door. "I just had a weird conversation with Sam. What happened after I left?"

Judy shook her head. "I didn't think your plan of leaving right after the speech was a good idea. But I was totally wrong. It actually went pretty well."

Steve pulled a chair to the edge of her desk and sat down. "I would have called, but I wanted to wait so I could talk to you in person. So, give me the details. I've been dying to know since I left."

"Okay." Judy turned her chair toward him and leaned forward. "So the room was dead quiet for about 15 seconds as soon as you left. Then Jennifer took over. Did you ask her to do that?"

Steve nodded and Judy smiled. "It seemed like you were behind that. So then Jennifer handed out a packet of papers with charts and graphs on most of the pages and showed everyone why the company was in such bad shape and why this plan was the absolute best way to fix it. Then she explained that we need three things to make it as a company."

"Really? What were they?"

Judy raised her eyebrows while adjusting her glasses. Steve noticed some gray streaks started to show in her blonde hair. "I know what they are, I just want to hear your interpretation of what Jennifer said."

"Well, she started by talking about keeping our customers happy and getting more work from them. She said that the plan, and the company for that matter, would crumble if we weren't getting enough work." Judy glanced at the ceiling, as if trying to remember more of what Jennifer had said. "She told us all that we need to take great care of our customers so they keep giving us more projects. She emphasized that everyone in the company is responsible for sales, not just you and the sales team."

"That explains why Sam was so interested in my appointment." Steve tapped Judy's desk. "I like that. Do you think they'll take it to heart?"

"I hope so." Judy searched in her desk and then found a pad of paper with notes scribbled on the top page. "Jennifer said this pay cut should change how we view the company. We are investing some of our time for free because we believe the company will be successful, and we need to take more ownership for the performance of the company. I liked how she said that the days of just doing your work and collecting a paycheck are over."

Steve nodded. "I really like that. How did the others respond?"

"You know, I was surprised." Judy shrugged, shaking her head again. "I thought we would get a lot of people complaining. But everybody just seemed grateful to still have a job. All of that was Jennifer's second point--the employees have to come together and take on this ownership attitude or everyone could end up out of a job."

Steve walked to Judy's window. A few more flowers were beginning to bloom in the landscape outside the office, spattering yellow and lavender in delicate patterns. "So, what was the third thing needed to survive?"

Judy consulted her notepad. "Find ways to cut costs. She actually opened it up and asked for some suggestions on what the company can do to save money, and she promised that the more we can save, the quicker we'll return to our regular salaries."

IMPACT INSIGHT #27
When all of the employees are interested in increasing sales, cutting costs, and the future of the company in general, silos between departments will be broken down, uniting the company.

"Great." Steve pumped his fist. "What suggestions were made?"

"You know, I can't remember them all. But Phil suggested everyone should stop using so much toilet paper so he can get his manager job back." Judy grinned. "It was actually quite funny--everyone laughed. Jennifer wrote all of the ideas down. I was too busy watching everyone and trying to get a read on what they were thinking."

"Do you think anyone will quit?" Steve didn't like putting his employees in the position to even consider quitting, but he knew he had no other choice.

"I think everyone has had that thought at least once so far today. But it seems like the employees are on board with the plan. The managers are hustling to reorganize the teams and even-out the project load on everyone. Things have come together well so far."

Steve moved from the window toward the door. "Thanks for the update, Judy. I know this hasn't been easy on you. I couldn't do it without you. By the way, have we removed the terminated employees from the server and inactivated their key cards?"

Judy held up a piece of paper from her desk. "It's all done, and the letters of recommendation, tailored to the traits and qualities you emailed me for each employee, will be ready for your signature by the end of the day." Steve thought about the range of emotions these terminated employees must have experienced, thanks to him.

Steve left, anxious to get to his laptop and respond to a few emails. He began to think about what a bad leader he'd been for the last several months. The stress of the whole situation blinded him from being effective. He felt even more grateful that Jennifer was helping him to snap out of that funk and make the tough decisions he'd been avoiding.

IMPACT INSIGHT #28
Even if they are only part-time, the CFO of entrepreneurial companies can significantly help the entrepreneur with all sorts of issues and problems.

While he walked he pulled out his iPhone and sent Jennifer a text: Sounds like u knocked it out of the park. Thx!

Steve sat at his desk and began to check his email. His phone buzzed a few minutes later with Jennifer's reply: Thx. Now we need 2 figure cash flow 4 next quarter. I'll be back Monday AM 2 start.

Now, if only things at home could take a turn for the better. But another weekend of trying to spend time and engage with his family, like Jeff advised, was mainly unsuccessful. His attempt to take Tyler driving turned into an argument with his son. Of course, Aubrye took Tyler's side. Even Emma, his youngest daughter who seemed the least affected by his failures, didn't seem interested in being around him. By Sunday, Steve found himself thinking about his business because at least he was having some success there. But he was still out of cash, and he looked forward to Jennifer helping him solve that problem next.

17

VALLEY

Monday finally felt like the first day of spring. The brown, dead grass began to yield a few blades of green. But it would still be months before the snow on the mountains melted. Steve felt some remorse for the people he had to let go, but the sense of new beginning was taking hold in his mind. Like the snow melting, he knew it would take some time to get Bolty all the way back on track.

Steve kept looking at the whiteboard in his office, anxious to solve his problems with the help of his CFO consultant.

	PROBLEM	SOLUTION
X	Barely made payroll	Monthly IMPACT Indicators
	Out of cash	Quarterly IMPACT Forecaster
	Key employees left	Daily/Weekly IMPACT Indicators
	Large customer left	Annual IMPACT Forecaster
	IRS, Lawsuit, Vision for future	5-Year IMPACT Forecaster
	Financial leader deficiencies	IMPACT CFO Services

Jennifer spent a good part of the day working with Judy, Dave, a programming manager, and Karen, the contract administrator and accounting assistant. Jennifer seemed a natural at working with others in a business environment. Steve could only imagine the rest of her clients appreciated her contributions to their businesses as much as he did to his.

While walking through his door, Jennifer spoke to Steve. "We've figured out exactly how bad problem number Two is. The clarity we gain from the Quarterly IMPACT Forecaster will now help us solve it."

Steve turned toward Jennifer, who sat in front of his desk. "Yeah, I'm very worried about cash flow. How bad is it?"

Jennifer opened her laptop and turned it toward the business owner. "We still have some short-term cash flow challenges. We won't start to feel the benefits of the payroll reductions for another couple of weeks, but the severance pay hurt our cash flow immediately. Add in the fact that we are starting a lot of new work that will take thirty days until we get paid, and we're definitely not out of the woods yet. I've put together this chart that shows our projected cash balance, week-by-week, for the next quarter."

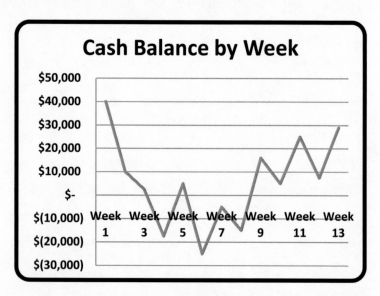

Jennifer pointed toward the chart on her laptop, specifically the steep slope that became negative in week Four and then bottomed out in week six. "You can see that we are headed toward a very tight month in terms of cash flow."

"A tight month." Steve inflected his voice, shifted his position in his chair, and began to feel uneasy with the downward trend he saw. "We're in the negative for all but one of the weeks, and even that week is barely positive. How are we going to survive that?"

Now Jennifer pointed toward the jagged trend upward at the right of the chart. "There is a positive in all of this. Look at week Nine and beyond. We'll be trending into positive cash flow, and it looks pretty sustainable based on the payroll cuts and when we are getting paid by our customers. This cash flow problem is really only about one month long. After that, it looks like it resolves itself."

Steve stood and began to pace. "But where am I going to get the cash to keep us afloat for the next two months. The line of credit at the bank is tapped out and I doubt anyone else will give me a loan. My credit score is probably shot thanks to being behind on all of my obligations as it is."

"I've already called the bank." Jennifer turned the laptop so it faced her again, glancing at her watch. "They're going to be here in about thirty minutes."

Steve stepped back and threw his hands up in the air. "You did what? Are you kidding? I've been trying to avoid the bank for the last month, and you've invited them to come here? What are you trying to do to me?"

"I know the people at your bank well, Steve." Jennifer's voice was firm, but still calm. "They're reasonable. Put yourself in their shoes. The more you avoid them, the less they trust you and the more they perceive you as a problem. Since they probably already think that, what will it hurt to be honest with them? I think you might be surprised how open they'll be to the story we have to tell. We're really headed in the right direction, with one last valley we've got to cross."

IMPACT INSIGHT #29
Building an honest, open relationship with your lending institution usually proves to be best for all parties.

Steve crossed his arms, wanting to be angry and kick Jennifer out. But he knew she was right. "I hope you know what you're doing. I'm afraid they'll come in here and shut me down."

Jennifer's hazel green eyes exuded confidence. "They certainly have the power to do that, but trust me when I say that's the last thing they want to do. Your line of credit is secured by your receivables, meaning if they did shut you down, they would have to collect money from all of your customers to get repaid. But you and I know that if they shut us down, they'll never be able to collect from the customers because we'll be in breach of contract, not having completed the work we promised to deliver. The bank really needs us to succeed, or they'll be in a very tough spot."

Steve considered this for a few moments. "I guess you're right. But what about my personal guarantee on the line of credit?" Steve considered this, then answered his own question. "I guess since the economy has wiped out all of the equity in my house and everything else I own, that wouldn't be a very profitable option for them either."

Jennifer nodded. "You see, the last thing they want to do is shut you down. They'll never get their money back if they do. So they're very interested in helping Bolty succeed. I know this will sound crazy to you, but I think I can get them to loan us the extra money we need to make it through the next two months."

IMPACT INSIGHT #30

Lending institutions usually secure collateral as a backup plan to recoup their money if an entrepreneur defaults on a loan. But they would always prefer the business be successful and pay them back in lieu of having to foreclose on or seize assets for which they probably can't get as much value as they need.

Steve sat down, shaking his head. "I'm one month behind on my payments to them, and you think you can get them to give me more money? Yeah, you must be crazy."

Jennifer smiled. "We need to give them a goodwill offering when they come. I'm talking about bringing the loan current with the payment we missed plus the one due this month. We can handle cutting them a check today. I included it in this forecast. May I have Judy prepare a check for them so you can sign it and give it to them when they arrive?

"I'm trusting you on this." Steve glared at Jennifer.

Jennifer turned her laptop so she could see the screen. "I have a few things to show them and discuss with them. It would be helpful if you could mention any noteworthy new projects we're starting in the next couple of months as well as generally instill some confidence in them about Bolty's future. They'll be here at 4 PM."

Steve looked at the calendar on his computer. "I need to leave by 4:30. I told my son I would be at his basketball game on the other side of town. I've broken too many promises at home because of this business, and I need to get that righted."

Jennifer's hazel green eyes softened. "I bet you've been spending every waking moment focusing on this business. I've seen other entrepreneurs get caught in a similar trap, and some have lost their families because of it. Sounds like you've got the right perspective on that, though."

"Not like it should be," Steve said. "But I'm trying to get better. Knowing we have no cash in four weeks sure makes it hard to go to his game, especially if being here will help us resolve that issue."

"No, you should go to the game. I don't think the meeting will take more than thirty minutes anyway." Jennifer stood and picked up her laptop. I'm going to set this up in the conference room. I'll let you know when they arrive."

"Thank you." Steve returned to working on a proposal for a prospective customer. *It's hard to focus on anything when I see, in a month from now, I'll have a negative bank balance on that graph. Jennifer is approaching this much differently than I would, but it's obvious I don't always do things the best way. I hope she knows what she's doing.*

A half-hour later, Jennifer poked her head through Steve's doorway. "They're here. Would you mind getting the check from Judy? I'll show them to the conference room."

Steve walked to Judy's office wondering why Jennifer referred to the bank as 'they' and 'them'. He had only worked with one person at the bank, a short, portly gentleman named Rich Pickens.

With the check in his left hand, Steve greeted Rich by shaking his hand. "Hello, Steve. It's been a little while." Rich adjusted the sleeve on his shirt and said, "Let me introduce you to our Chief Credit Officer, Zach Grant." *Now I understand why Jennifer referred to the bank in plural form. I guess it takes at least two to form a firing squad*, which is what Steve felt like he was putting himself in front of.

Zach, a tall, broad-shouldered man with thick brown hair stuck his enormous hand out and Steve shook it. "So how is the banking business these days?"

"As you know, we're a small community bank." Zach pulled a business card from his pocket, handing it to Steve. "We've mostly avoided the effects of the struggling economy, although we're still concerned about some of the loans in our portfolio."

Jennifer invited everyone to sit down. "Rich and Zach, thanks for coming over. We have some things we need to cover with you, but first we need to give you this." Jennifer glanced at Steve, and Steve handed Rich the check. "This should bring us current."

"Thank you," Rich said. "We were starting to get a little worried about Bolty. How are things going?"

Jennifer took over. Referencing some charts and graphs projected on the screen, she talked about current ratio, gross margin, backlog, cash flow, borrowing base, days sales outstanding, and more. The two men asked questions like pitchers throwing fastballs to a batter. Jennifer answered succinctly by hitting their pitches sharply, balls spraying all over the field and a few even out of the park. *She has these guys on the edge of their seats, eating out of the palm of her hand. Wish I'd thought of this.*

After about five minutes Jennifer invited Steve to address the future prospects of the company. Steve cleared his throat. "We're seeing activity for our services increase, and we think we're well-positioned to capitalize on that. In fact, earlier today we were awarded a project from a brand new customer."

Jennifer moved the mouse to her laptop a few times. "But we have a cash challenge in the next few months that we need to solve." She projected the chart she had showed Steve earlier on the screen. Steve's entire body tensed with the fear of exposing too much information to these finance-savvy bankers.

Jennifer stood and approached the screen. She pointed at the negative and then positive trends in Bolty's cash flow and explained what was causing each in terms the bankers readily digested. She also talked to them about the working capital cycle of the business and how she had pushed it to its very limit just to make the last payroll. "So, to estimate on the safe side, we need about another $30,000 to make it through the next two months. Then we should be able to use internal cash to get this business all the way back on track."

Rich and Zach looked at each other, then Zach, clearly the higher ranking officer of the bank, spoke first. "Jennifer, this will be very tough to sell to our loan committee. I sit on that committee, and the fact that Bolty missed a payment will not be looked upon favorably."

Steve cringed, thinking this would be the part of the conversation where the bankers decided to never do business with Bolty again. Jennifer smiled. *What on earth is she smiling for?*

"Zach, I think it's much simpler than that," Jennifer said. "You've put a very strict loan covenant in place on concentration of the receivables. In fact, I bet 5% is lower than almost any other customer you have, is that correct?"

Zach looked at the table, then back at Jennifer. "That's correct. But we were concerned that with so few customers, we could get burned if just one of them went out of business."

Jennifer sat up. "Did you even look at the customer list? These are multi-billion dollar companies that aren't going anywhere, especially into bankruptcy. I'm proposing you raise the concentration percentage to 20%, which is about the average for lines of credit, from what I've seen. That will immediately buy us about $42,000 in extra capacity on the line of credit, which is still below the upper limit you and your committee approved less than a year ago."

Zach leaned back, looking like a boxer confused by the series of jabs, hooks, and upper-cuts he was being dealt, while Rich said, "Maybe we should go ahead and get your line renewed and just include that change to the loan covenant." Steve relaxed, Rich turning to his superior, Zach, to make sure he hadn't suggested something inappropriate. "How would the committee look at that?"

"I like that idea, Rich." Zach seemed warmer, almost comfortable. "The bank is very concerned with its current customers. In fact, we're not actively looking for new ones right now. We're trying to shore up the business we have and keep from having to write off too many loans. With the clarity of your plan in front of us, it seems like renewing the line will get you exactly what you need to turn the corner in the business. We need to help you with that if we can."

Like an opportunistic sports franchise owner, about to trade for their in-conference rival's best player, Jennifer seemed to sense the discussion was going in Bolty's favor. "I think we'd be very interested to move the renewal up a little to facilitate this. Steve, would you agree?"

Steve could not believe what he was witnessing. He suspected Jennifer had planned how this meeting would go long before it ever started. "Yes, I'm fine with renewing now."

Jennifer turned toward the bankers. "Rich, what do you need from me to prepare the renewal?"

"Jennifer, these reports will be all I need for my write-up for the committee." Rich held up a packet of papers Jennifer had prepared for the bank and had handed to Rich earlier in the meeting. "Your Monthly IMPACT Indicators and the Quarterly IMPACT Forecaster are very impressive. I wish all of the bank's customers had reporting like this."

"Thanks," Jennifer said. "Well, I know we all have things to do, so I'll forward them over to you in electronic format and then follow-up in a few days." She looked at Zach. "Are there any other concerns you think the loan committee might have?"

Zach shook his head. "Not that hasn't already been answered in what you've prepared. The backlog trend and the payroll reduction plan you have executed will be well-received."

"OK, then I look forward to talking to you in a few days." Jennifer stood, followed by the others in the room. Everyone shook hands and Steve noticed his palms were not quite as damp as they had been in earlier weeks.

Rich spoke as the group walked to the lobby. "Steve, I think hiring Jennifer is one of the smartest moves you've made. The information she presented today helps the bank have a great deal of confidence in Bolty's future."

After a little more conversation, the bankers left and Jennifer followed Steve back to his office.

"You had that entire meeting planned out before it even happened, didn't you?" Steve quizzed Jennifer, whose face had a small, almost secretive smile.

"Pretty much." Jennifer pulled on the tails of her white shirt to straighten it. "We had four things going for us." With each point, she held up another finger. "One, they need to help us get through this short-term crunch or their entire loan balance is at risk. Two, the receivables concentration they imposed on Bolty was very unfair, and they know it. Zach was very uncomfortable that I called him out on it, too. Third, they left with a check that brings the relationship current with a clear plan to keep it current moving forward. And fourth, Rich is hungry for the commission he'll earn for renewing the line of credit. With his bank bringing on no new business, he's trying to survive in banking."

IMPACT INSIGHT #31
A CFO knows how bankers think and what is important to them. Entrepreneurs who don't have a CFO are at a disadvantage when trying to work with bankers and lending institutions.

Steve closed his laptop and started gathering some papers and files. "Very well done. I owe you an apology for flipping out when I found out they were coming here. That went much better than I expected." Steve chuckled. "Now I'm off to a basketball game. Thanks for your help."

"You're welcome. Working on keeping key employees is next on the list. I'll be back on Thursday to start on that." Jennifer returned to the conference room.

Steve unplugged his laptop and put it in his bag. Another day survived, he exited the building and went to his car. His phone buzzed with a message from Aubrye.

She texted: Don't 4get Tyler's game.

He texted back: On my way.

Not that I deserve any, but she really has no confidence in me anymore. I'm pitiful.

As he drove across town to the basketball gym where Tyler would play, he felt some of his confidence coming back, and it felt great. But he worried if he could make any progress with his family. *It's just like the snow on the mountains. My family has put up snow barriers between me and them. I just need to give it some more time, and then hopefully the barriers they've put up will melt away.*

18

CONFRONTATION

Steve arrived at Tyler's game just after tip-off. Smelling like a combination of teenage sweat and wood floor cleaner, the gym was cool and loud. Steve walked to the visitors' side and briefly looked for Aubrye and his three girls. Then he remembered they were at the elementary school's annual Spring fundraiser. Aubrye was serving a term as the PTA president, which meant she was in charge of the entire event. Although initially reluctant to take the volunteer leadership position, she had decided it would give her something to do since she left the University while still spending time with the kids.

Steve smiled as he thought about the positive influence his wife was having on the teachers and students involved in the public institution of learning attended by all three of his daughters. With a doctorate in education and a wealth of experience in the field, Aubrye was probably more qualified to run the school than the principal.

Undistracted by the rest of his family and as his son's entire cheering section, he watched Tyler closely. *He's a lot taller than most of the other kids, and he's also got the longest hair. I wish he'd keep it shorter, but he refuses to get it cut. He's really improved since last year, and he's bounced back from his biking accident quite well. He's got confidence and he responds to his new coach. I wonder how I can get him to respond so positively to me.*

By the end of the third quarter the Alta Hawks, Tyler's team, had pulled ahead of the opposition by 30 points. The coach sat his starting players and went to the depths of his bench to field his team on the floor for the rest of the game. Steve watched Tyler talk and joke with the other players, especially the young man sitting to Tyler's left with a #22 jersey, as they enjoyed their blowout victory and cheered on their teammates who rarely saw action. *I wonder if that is one of Tyler's good friends he's always texting. A better father would know these things.*

Steve got an idea, and as soon as the game was over he approached Tyler before the team went to the locker room. "Hey Tyler, do you want to drive home with me?" Steve spoke loud enough to overcome the echoing chatter in the gym. "You can drive."

Tyler spun around. "For real?"

"Yeah. Will your coach let you go home with me, or do you have to ride with the team on the bus?"

Tyler ran to Coach Smith, who's freshly shaved bald head and reddish-brown goatee made him look distinguished and lively. Steve guessed the coach was probably in his mid-thirties. The two talked briefly, then Tyler turned toward Steve and simultaneously gave a head-nod and a thumbs-up. He jogged to the locker room and hollered over his shoulder to Steve. "I'll meet you in the parking lot in a minute."

As Steve exited the building and walked to his car, he thought about Jeff's advice to engage with his family. He had encouraged Steve to really listen and put all worries and concerns about the business aside. *I can do this. But it sure feels weird to sit in the passenger seat. I'm sure glad there's no ice on the roads.* He chuckled. *Now maybe we can make it home in one piece.*

Steve texted Aubrye: Tyler won. Do u want me to pick up dinner on way home?

She texted back: K. Pizza's fine.

Tyler opened the door, threw his bag into the back, and then hopped into the driver's seat. His black, long hair still a little sweaty, he put on his seatbelt and grabbed the steering wheel. "I like driving your sedan much more than Mom's bulky SUV." He winked at his dad. "Especially now that it has a bathtub hood."

"Let's try to stay off the sidewalks this time." Steve tried to sound like he was teasing, hiding how serious he actually was. "Seems like you get along really well with the new coach."

Tyler laughed. "When we're winning. He's kind of a jerk when we're losing. Luckily that hasn't happened too many times this year."

"Well, your whole team was playing lights-out basketball tonight. It was fun to watch. When was the last time you guys played that well?"

Tyler flipped the blinker on and changed lanes, using his mirrors and checking his blind spot like a pro. "It's been a long time. I hope my Utah Jazz play like that when I go to their game for my birthday in a few weeks."

"You're going to the game?" Steve usually was in charge of taking the family to games, so he was surprised plans were made without his involvement.

"Duh. Mom hooked me up with two front-row seats. I'm taking Brandon and we're going to watch the Jazz school the Boston Celtics."

Steve's heartbeat accelerated and he turned the vent on, suddenly feeling warm. "You guys will have a great time, except I heard the Celtics are pretty good this year. Hopefully you won't let a Jazz loss spoil your birthday." Steve tried to keep things light to mask his anger toward Aubrye for spending so lavishly on their son's birthday present. Thanks to the stack of unpaid medical bills from Tyler's mountain biking accident and Steve's newly-reduced salary, he couldn't see how they could afford such a gift.

Tyler offered to go inside the restaurant to get the pizza when they stopped. When he returned, the car quickly filled with the smell of hot pizza and cardboard, a welcome scent for Steve. The drive went quicker than expected, and Tyler didn't get mad at him once. *Will this be my first victory engaging with someone from my family?*

As Tyler pulled the car into the garage, Steve saw the severely dented hood of Aubrye's SUV. Although his back hadn't ached all day, he felt a twinge of pain.

Tyler burst into the house, clearly energized by both his team's victory and the freedom he felt behind the wheel. Steve followed with two boxes of pizza. Aubrye was setting the table for a late dinner. Zoe, still sporting her blue and white Tiger basketball uniform from her 6th grade recreation league team from her game before the fundraiser, was carefully placing cups next to each paper plate. Stacey, the ten-year-old, carried a pitcher to the table, her black braids laying down her back like two velvet ribbons. And Emma, dressed in a pink tutu and oddly, a blue Gap hoodie, was doing twirls in the far corner of the kitchen while waving white paper napkins over her head.

Steve tried to be proactive. "What can Tyler and I do to help?"

Aubrye looked up, her dark curly hair still hanging over the table. "Tyler needs to take his stinky uniform straight to the laundry room. And you can put the pizzas on the table. We're ready to eat."

Tyler went upstairs and the girls washed their hands. Tyler came back, sporting gray sweats and a black t-shirt, and for the first time in quite a while, it looked like the entire family was going to eat together. With Steve's energy and focus on the business and all of the kids' activities, family dinners together were a very rare occurrence, if they even happened at all.

Steve sat at the head of the rectangular table, directly across from Aubrye who was at the other end. Emma began to sit down. She looked at her mom, then her dad, then back at her mom. Then she sat next to Steve. *Things are definitely going my way with the family.* The rest of the kids each took a place at the table.

With a quick blessing offered over the food, everyone began talking about the highlights of the day. Steve couldn't help but stew over Aubrye's spending. It seemed like blatant disregard for everything he was trying to accomplish for the family. A few minutes into the meal, Steve found a non-confrontational way to bring it up. "Aubrye, did you get the estimate on the costs to repair my incident with your vehicle?"

Aubrye filled her cup with water from the pitcher on the table, and then began filling everyone else's. "Yes, and it wasn't good. They said I would need a new hood, and it will cost at least $2,750. And the insurance company said they're not going to pay."

Steve thought the kids would look at their mom, overwhelmed with sticker-shock. Instead, they were all looking at him, probably more interested in his reaction. "That's a lot of money, especially considering the doctor and hospital bills and the fact that our income is going to go down."

Other than Emma humming the tune to a song she learned in school, the room was silent. Zoe shifted in her seat.

"And I have no idea how we're going to afford that and Tyler's Jazz tickets." Steve immediately sensed Aubrye would be upset with what he said, but it was too late.

Aubrye looked at Tyler, who shrugged his shoulders, raised his eyebrows, and tilted his head to the right, as if to apologize for telling his dad about the tickets.

Aubrye tightened her lips, causing a few wrinkles to appear around her mouth. "I bought those tickets before I knew anything about the cut in your pay. And I certainly can't drive around without a hood on my car--the one you fell on is about to come all the way off."

Emma started poking Stacey, who repeated 'Stop it' each time. Zoe stirred her cup of water with a plastic knife. Tyler kept eating, seeming to be more concerned with the pizza than the fight that was breaking out right in front of him.

Aubrye raised her voice, deliberately pronouncing each syllable in an angry voice. "Emma, will you please stop poking your sister?"

Emma pulled her hand to her chest and held it with the other. Every muscle in Steve's body tensed. "Well, I don't know how to pay for all of this. We just can't seem to get ahead, or even tread water for that matter. We're sinking, and these extra expenses aren't helping; they're just bringing water into the boat faster."

Tyler stood up. "I'll sell the dumb tickets to someone else then. Whatever."

"You're not selling the tickets." Aubrye lowered her voice's pitch but not volume. "Those are for your birthday, and besides, this is not about the tickets. Steve, this is neither the time nor the place to do this."

"Oh, really?" Steve's voice began to rise. "Like allowing Zoe to overhear your gripe session with your sister is the right time or place?" Steve stood and began to walk to his office.

"Hiding in there isn't going to solve anything," Aubrye blurted, anger oozing from her words.

Steve stopped and turned around. "Yeah, and telling me to focus on fixing the business and then turning around and telling people that I only care about the business sure isn't going to solve much either."

Tyler motioned for all of the kids to leave the room. They picked up their plates and Tyler grabbed a box of pizza. All of the children quickly disappeared upstairs, more silent than if they were all asleep.

Tears began to well in Aubrye's eyes and her nose began to run. "I didn't know she heard that. But that's not the point. I never told you to neglect us. How could you think I meant that? Why can't you do both--fix the business and still not shut us out?"

Steve raised his voice even louder. "You're so hypocritical. I can't read between the lines and interpret everything you say. At least I've been trying to do something to make this work. You've just given up on me, and I'm tired of trying to figure out what you want from me."

Aubrye shook her head, the same way she would if someone was telling her something that she knew wasn't true. "How in the world would fixing this business help the family? I could care less if that business fails. But I do care if this family fails. And your whacked out perspective is messing everything up."

Trading blows with Aubrye, Steve felt like a fighter who was getting punched more than he could punch back. He was taking a beating from a boxer half his size but smarter and more skilled. But Jeff's words about really listening to his wife kept playing in his mind. *Maybe I need to read between the lines. What is she trying to tell me? Did she not mean what she said about me fixing the business first? But she said my perspective was 'whacked-out'.*

Aubrye, gathering more ammunition, barked, "You eat, sleep, and drink that business. You give us absolutely no reason to think you even want to be part of this family. Other than your twisted view of reality, why would you think saving your stupid business would have anything to do with keeping this family together?"

Steve let down his gloves and exposed his body and head to his opposition. In his loudest voice, he forced himself to say something he never wanted to admit. "Because I was somehow under the impression that you and the kids would reject me if the business failed. Okay? I said it. I'm so afraid of failure it's paralyzed me."

Steve looked at the ground, which is where he figured he'd be laying soon. *I've set her up for the knockout punch. It's all over for me.*

Aubrye stood motionless. Exposed, Steve was very uncomfortable, like he was in front of a large audience in his underwear. *All those daytime talk shows tell you to get your feelings out and then you'll feel better. Yeah right.*

Tormented by the silence of his wife after sharing such a private weakness, Steve spoke just to fill the room with something other than his self-conscious discomfort. "I don't think I would know who I was if I lost my business. I feel the same way about my family, but my fear of failure blinded me."

Steve's head began to hurt and he felt like he was drowning in his failures. He began to pace in front of his office as he ran his fingers through his hair, pressing hard against his scalp to try and ease the pain in his head.

After several more seconds of silence, Aubrye spoke. "I think you justified tuning us out by thinking that I somehow authorized you to do it."

Steve continued pacing. He wanted to be angry at Aubrye for analyzing him, but he felt too overwhelmed to put up any more of a fight. *After all, she's right.*

Aubrye's volume dropped several notches. "Look, we need to talk about this, but we also have four very frightened kids upstairs pretending to eat pizza but who are really trying to secretly listen to us. Is there any way we can finish our conversation after we get everyone to bed?"

> **IMPACT INSIGHT #32**
> *Starting, nurturing, and growing a business is like raising a child, and entrepreneurs often allow the business to become an important part of their identity, just like proud parents do with their kids.*

Steve shook his head. "Conversation? That, my dear wife, was a fight, and I lost. Again." Steve knew he was being a jerk, but he'd felt like he'd just taken several jabs to the body and head, with a couple of punishing left hooks mixed in. "I don't think I can face the kids. I feel like such a failure."

Aubrye looked at Steve the same way she looks at Tyler whenever he makes an excuse for not doing his chores. "Steve, you need to face them. It's the only way to move past this."

Steve looked at the floor. "I can't. This is too much for me to handle."

Aubrye scowled at Steve. "I'm going to try and smooth this over with our children--alone. I'm telling you this right now, Mr. Steve Loveland. You better get yourself pulled together. This family can't take any more eruptions like tonight, and my patience is gone." She stormed up the stairs.

Like a dog scolded by his master, Steve dropped his head and trudged to the home office. He wished he could erase all of his mistakes and immediately fix everything. But he remembered the melting snowpack on the top of the mountain. He would need to change his behavior to get his family to thaw first, and then eventually warm up to him again.

19
SCOREBOARD

A couple of hours passed before Aubrye entered the home office where Steve was trying to review the last few weeks' worth of proposals his sales reps had done, noticing more bids than normal for the complex type of work Bolty wanted. But he found it hard to concentrate on anything after he revealed such a painful, private feeling. She stopped at his door, not seeming to want to come all the way in.

"I think this is going to be a long conversation, so you might as well come in and make yourself comfortable on the old couch." Steve looked at what had been his bed more often than not recently. Aubrye moved toward the couch, passing Steve just close enough that he could smell her perfume.

They talked until early in the morning, and it was possibly their most excruciatingly honest yet most productive discussion ever. Aubrye was right--Steve's eruption had nothing to do with basketball tickets and everything to do with a complete breakdown in communication between the couple. Steve apologized for not making his family a priority, and Aubrye even apologized for being insensitive to everything he was going through.

Aubrye explained that she was tired of parenting alone, and she wanted her husband back. And not the husband that was always so distracted, but the one that she fell in love with and married--funny, thoughtful, and even occasionally charming.

Steve faced the reality that he had projected things onto Aubrye that she never thought, specifically that she had somehow endorsed his recent behavior of neglecting the family to try and save Bolty. "At some point you have to realize that even if you lose the business you won't lose us." Aubrye reached from the couch and touched Steve's hand for a moment. "We'll be here for you, through thick and thin."

The more they talked, the more Steve softened. He looked at Aubrye and, for the first time in a while, he didn't see an enemy or someone trying to pull him down or add to his burden. She never was the enemy, but Steve had somehow started to feel that way. He saw the woman he loved, who had captivated his heart so fully when they first met seventeen years earlier he didn't go on a single date with another woman ever again.

They decided that they would scale their spending down as much as possible, hopeful Aubrye could continue to be with the kids rather than return to teaching at the University.

The next few days went much better, with Steve mentally turning off the business for a few hours every night. He apologized to the kids for his outburst, and they seemed willing to forgive. Thursday morning came, and Steve was anticipating his interaction with Jennifer. He studied the list on the whiteboard and was pleased two of his biggest problems were solved. *Only four to go.*

Jennifer walked through Steve's door and sat in what was becoming her usual chair. Always professionally dressed, she appeared ready to get to work. "We've got some good stuff to cover today."

Steve hit send on the email he had just finished. "Good. I'm ready for it."

Jennifer held a silver ballpoint pen in her hand. "You've been in this business for over a decade. I'm sure you've had many great days, horrible days, and mediocre days. I realize you'd probably say more horrible days recently, but I'm talking about the entire life of the company. Here's my question--how do you know if you win or lose each day in this business?"

"Any number of things can determine that." Steve moved the mouse connected to his laptop, closing his email program. "Like the new project we were awarded yesterday that will cover about half of one month's overhead. That made yesterday a huge victory."

Steve thought for a few seconds. "Some of the other indicators might be if we collect an old receivable. Or, if we receive a positive customer testimonial. Or, if an employee thanks me for her job. I have a lot more I could mention. Is that what you're after?"

"Yes." Jennifer lightly set her pen on Steve's desk. "Now, did you notice a common theme among all of the things you mentioned?"

Steve looked at the ceiling. "No. Not really."

"Each one of them is a qualitative measurement that may or may not actually be good for the business." With a hand on each arm rest, Jennifer pushed herself back into the chair, now sitting up tall and straight. "So, landing that new large project is fantastic, but what if its rock-bottom price will cost you money to complete it. Collecting on an old receivable is always welcome, but what if you had to write-off 50% of it to get the customer to pay anything? Having an employee thank you for their job is nice, but what if she just stole $10,000 from the company? I'm not trying to be negative, just cast into light that good and bad, terrible and great are being viewed pretty subjectively right now."

Feeling defensive, Steve sat up, folded his arms, and tilted his head forward. "Aren't your what/if scenarios a little dramatic?"

"Sure they are, but only to make my point." Jennifer held the index finger and thumb on her right hand about two inches apart. "When your company was young and had just a few employees, you intrinsically knew how to judge if each thing that happened was good or bad." Jennifer now held her left and right hand about three feet apart. "But now that you have dozens of employees, lots of customers, and several different complex service offerings, are you 100% sure that none of my dramatic what/if's are true?"

"No, I guess I'm not." Steve consented.

Jennifer crossed her legs and leaned forward slightly. "The fact that you've grown Bolty to where you're no longer able to know every detail about it is definitely not a bad thing. However, not having a way to quantitatively define, manage, and report on it as though you were in every detail is usually problematic."

Steve cupped his right hand under his chin. "I think I understand what you're saying, but I'm still unclear on what I'm supposed to do with it."

Jennifer raised her arms to stretch her back. "What I'm ultimately interested in is how we can answer the win or lose question, of course meeting the IMPACT criteria, every day."

"Come to think of it, I really don't have a scoreboard for each day. What would we need on that scoreboard to give me the right picture of my daily performance?" Steve studied his whiteboard as though it might give him an answer.

Jennifer began to push her pen, forward and back. "My job today is to help us figure that out. So, let's talk through a few things together."

"Okay." Steve wondered if this discussion would make him feel better or defensive, like he had a minute before.

"I want you to explain your business model to me. How do you make money? And I'm not looking for the answer 'satisfying customers' – that's a given. How do all of the moving parts of your business work together to create value – cash and profit?" Jennifer picked up her pen and began rolling it back and forth in her hand.

> **IMPACT INSIGHT #33**
> *At the core of the daily business scoreboard should be the key elements of the business model--how the company makes money.*

Steve reminisced to his days in business school. His professors would theorize about business models, but they had no clue what they were talking about compared to all of the real-world business people with whom he had associated since walking the campus of Pepperdine University. "We give a fixed price to our customers for each project, and then we have to make sure we keep our promises to them while we keep our internal costs for their project as low as possible. We keep whatever is left over."

"So, tell me about these 'internal costs'? What are they, and how do we keep them low?"

"You know the answer to these questions?" Steve liked to question the intentions of his consultant, knowing that she had certain outcomes already planned for this discussion. "Why are you asking me?"

Jennifer continued to work the pen in her hand. "It's worthwhile for us to go through this exercise, Steve. Bear with me, I do have a point."

Steve rubbed his hands together, trusting that Jennifer knew what she was doing. "Well, our main cost for each of our projects is payroll. When we bid on a project, we estimate the amount of time we think each project will take and we try to apply the cost of the employees that we will most likely assign to the project to that time. Controlling our internal costs really has to do with keeping our employees at or below their budgeted hours on each project."

Jennifer attempted to summarize. "So, the success or failure of each project is determined by how accurately you bid a project and then how well you live within the budgeted hours for that project. Does that sound right?"

"Yes, it does." Steve placed both hands on the edge of his desk, tipping his chair back momentarily. "So, is this what you mean by business model?"

"Being profitable on our projects is the first of three parts of our model." Jennifer drew a round circle on a paper and split it into thirds, writing 'profit projects' in one section. "The second part has to do with having enough profitable work each day that we can cover our overhead and maybe even have a little extra left for you at the end—net profit."

Jennifer filled in the second section with 'daily workload' and then put 'backlog' in the remaining third. "The third part has to do with our future work, or backlog. The more we have, the more flexible we can be in some of our pricing decisions."

Steve nodded his head. "Yeah, boiled down, that's my business model. And it's the same for a lot of other companies, too."

"Now Steve, do you remember the question that I asked that prompted this entire conversation?"

Steve tapped the edge of his desk, as if to emphasize his answer. "Yes--how do I know if I win or lose each day?"

Jennifer set her pen on Steve's desk again and walked to the whiteboard. "The answer to that question lies in how well you executed your business model for that day. Period." She pointed at 'Key employees left'. "Right now Bolty does not have this daily, or weekly for that matter, reporting in place. But the motivation for getting it in place has as much to do with retaining your key employees as it does giving you the clarity you need to run Bolty."

Steve scratched his head. "I don't understand that. I thought all of these reports were for me to improve my business. What does this have to do with my employees?"

Steve's phone buzzed with a text message. It was from Aubrye. "Sorry Jennifer. Let me just respond to this text from my wife."

His phone in his hand, Steve read Aubrye's text: b on time 4 Tyler's b-day with ur parents 2night.

Steve hated being told what to do, especially when Aubrye treated him like a child, telling him everything he should and shouldn't do with a little bit of guilt-trip mixed in.

Steve replied: K.

He set his phone on the desk gently, although he wanted to throw it through his window. *Mental note to self: next time I have a long talk with Aubrye like last night, ask her as nicely as possible not to send texts that make it sound like she's my mother.* Pushing back his emotions, he looked back at Jennifer to let her know he was finished.

PROBLEM		SOLUTION
X	Barely made payroll	Monthly IMPACT Indicators
X	Out of cash	Quarterly IMPACT Forecaster
	Key employees left	Daily/Weekly IMPACT Indicators
	Large customer left	Annual IMPACT Forecaster
	IRS, Lawsuit, Vision for future	5-Year IMPACT Forecaster
	Financial leader deficiencies	IMPACT CFO Services

Jennifer underlined 'Key employees left' on the board with a red marker. "When I asked you if you knew if you won or lost each day, you could not give me a definitive answer—an answer that met the quantitative IMPACT criteria. Think about it. If you couldn't tell me what you needed to do to win, then I'm sure your employees don't know what they're supposed to do to in their daily jobs to help the company win."

Steve felt warm and walked to the thermostat just outside his office. He turned it down two degrees, then moved back to his desk. "Are you saying my employees don't know what to do every day?"

"Not exactly." Jennifer leaned against the wall next to the board, facing Steve. "Let's look at it this way. If we called one of your programmers into your office and asked him how he knows if he succeeded or failed at his job today, what do you think would be his answer?"

Steve thought for a few silent seconds. "Honestly, I think most of them would talk about getting their work done as quickly as possible and hope someone else doesn't mess it up."

"So, without the employees understanding the overall vision of how their work contributes to the success of the company, they tend to focus on basic task completion. No vision. Nothing to get excited about."

Steve was uncomfortable with how Jennifer was characterizing his company. "Wait a minute. We have company barbecues and parties. We try to make this a fun place to work."

Jennifer took a step toward Steve. "I get that. But no one in this company is passionate about helping it become great. And I think it's because they don't know how to. And the place to start is by teaching them how to win at their jobs every day and every week. Without a scoreboard, they don't even know who to root for."

Steve felt the cool air blow through the vent right above his desk onto his head and neck. "I think I need an example of how this might work."

"Okay, let's imagine we ask an employee about winning or losing each day. Her response talks about her efforts only, no mention of her coworkers or Bolty."

Jennifer lifted her hands like they were around an imaginary ball, a gesture she seemed to commonly use. "Then we take that same employee and teach her what the company is trying to accomplish each day and how she, individually, and her coworkers, collectively, can help Bolty hit its goals. Maybe we even offer her a little bonus if she wins and the company wins often enough? Will she have the clarity she needs? Will she start thinking about more than just herself? Will she become more engaged and possibly even passionate about what the company is trying to do?"

Steve sat up. "Actually, I bet she would try harder to work with the other team members on her projects to make sure she wasn't doing anything to slow them down. She would definitely start to think of something more than just her little part of the world."

"Exactly." Jennifer smiled. "Working at a job where you don't feel a part of something bigger than just yourself is not a lot of fun. Being involved in something you believe in, and feeling like you are an important contributing member to its success, now that's a place most people want to work."

Steve cringed, sensing he was about to be reminded how poorly he had been running his company. Jennifer took one step back, putting her next to the whiteboard again. "Is it too forward for me to suggest that perhaps part of the reason the key employees left was because they didn't have a vision of their role in helping Bolty succeed?"

Steve felt enlightened, yet he was tired of feeling like the poster child for how not to do what Jennifer was teaching. There was nothing Jennifer said that he didn't intuitively know, but he had never been able to see it as clearly as he did now.

Jennifer returned to her chair. "So, our next step is to get the Daily and Weekly IMPACT Indicators in place for your direct use as well as for the rest of the employees to have something they can get behind."

"How long do you think that will take?" Steve was pleased with the progress Jennifer had made, but was anxious to move through the rest of his list and stop making so many mistakes.

"Probably Wednesday of next week for the daily report, and then another week after that for the weekly report. I'm going to go and get started, if that's all right with you."

Steve decided he could wait that long. "Great. I love how we are moving through this list."

Jennifer smiled. "Yeah, I thought you would."

20
DAILY

Almost a week passed. Steve continued to spend undistracted time with his family in the evenings, and his relationships were improving. Even Aubrye's texts had warmed up a bit, which he appreciated. However, similar to expecting a feast and only being served bread and butter, he felt like something was missing, and he wanted more.

Jennifer had been in the office a few times working on the next set of reports. Today she had gathered Judy and all five of the engineering and programming managers in the conference room. Steve felt a little uncomfortable not being involved in the meeting, but he was also glad to use his time to try and land more work. And it was paying off. With a large project awarded last week and two more about to close, Steve was feeling more and more confident in Bolty's future.

"Steve, we're ready for you." Jennifer stuck her head through Steve's doorway. "Please come join us as soon as you can." She headed back to where the others were assembled.

Steve saved the document he was working on, then walked to the conference room. He thought about the day before when Sam Davenport, his long-time employee who had worked up to be a manager, paid him a brief visit, shaggy beard and all. Not only did Sam have positive comments about the hiring of Jennifer, he was also excited about the new reporting tool he was helping create. "These reports are going to be very valuable in the way we run the projects. This is one of the best things we've done in years," Sam had said.

Coming from Sam, that was especially meaningful to Steve. Steve knew that if one of his most tenured employees approved of the results of this initiative, then it was likely something beneficial. *That stubborn guy is never an easy sell if it means he has to change in the slightest way.*

As he arrived, Steve surveyed his managers. The four men and one woman were sitting around the long rectangular table looking quite proud of themselves. Judy was studying a packet of papers in front of her and Jennifer was focusing the projector, which illuminated her laptop display onto the screen at the far end of the room.

Steve sat in between Judy and Sam. "So, I'm curious to see what all of you have been up to."

All five managers and Judy looked to Jennifer, so Steve did the same. "I think we've got the Daily IMPACT Indicators ready to present to you." Judy passed a bottled water to Steve, and he noticed everyone else already had one. "We're going to show you how this report will make a difference in the performance of this company, and, more importantly, help the employees understand their roles in helping the company succeed."

Steve almost expected his managers to not be unified without his involvement in the process of implementing this report. He was, however, surprised and even a little offended that they seemed to be excited about the result of their efforts. He remembered Jennifer's comments about the impossibility of trying to be involved in every detail of a company the size of Bolty. He was glad they had accomplished this without him.

"Everyone here has been essential in completing this project." Jennifer sounded like a leader, praising the team in public and helping them stay motivated to make positive contributions to the company. "And everyone here is critical in implementing this new daily reporting tool in the future. Also, I want to remind everyone about keeping all of this information confidential. We should never share it with anyone outside of the company and only those who are approved to see it inside the company."

All of the managers nodded.

Jennifer stood and moved to the left of the screen. "In the past, we haven't had a way to clearly see if we're accomplishing what we need to as an entire business each day. Most of the employees have generally had a good idea of what they needed to be doing, but we lacked a measurement tool that could help everyone know how their efforts were contributing to the whole. So, what is it that we need to measure? What information is the most important to Bolty each day? What determines if we win or lose?"

Jennifer looked at Steve. "Steve, everybody else in here knows the answer. We've been working on it all week. We want to see if it takes you as long." Everyone in the room gave a nervous laugh as the employees watched for Steve's reaction to being put on the spot.

Pretending to not know the answer, Steve looked at the ceiling while lowering his eyebrows. Then he let a sly smile out. "This has everything to do with executing our business model, the way we make money." Steve felt a cough coming, so he quickly took a drink from his water bottle, then finished what he was saying. "And, for Bolty, we live and die by coming in at or below our budgeted labor costs on our projects. I think the most important number to know each day is if we made enough money on each of our projects."

A few managers sighed and Sam even reached over to pound knuckles with his boss. "So, when are you going to ask me a hard question?" The room erupted with laughter.

Jennifer, still smiling, moved toward the conference table and took a drink of water. "Okay Mr. Showoff. Here's a hard one. What are the main barriers to being able to see this information every day?"

Steve cleared his throat. "Employee time. Getting time turned in every day that is coded accurately to each job. And not creating so much busy work trying to track it all that it isn't worth the effort to collect the information in the first place."

Jennifer turned to the whiteboard and picked up the green marker, pulled the cap off, and wrote Steve's answer. "What you just described is no easy task, and no one in this room initially thought we could figure it out."

"I was definitely the most skeptical." Sam pulled at his beard, which always annoyed Steve.

"Yes, I would agree with that." Jennifer smiled at Sam. "But no one else was excited about it either, mainly because it meant we had to get everyone's time turned in every day, a significant change from weekly."

"Yes, it's a significant change, but it sure will help with the accuracy problem." Judy's voice was as passionate as Steve had ever heard it. No question she's in favor of all of this. She had been frustrated for years that employees recklessly just put their hours into projects without really accounting for how they actually spent their time. In fact, as the sole-enforcer of the weekly timesheet, Judy had often stood next to employees on the timesheet due date while they pencil-whipped their best recollection of the prior week.

Every time this subject had been discussed previously, he couldn't get past the administrative nightmare daily time collection would cause. "What about all the extra paperwork these daily timesheets will generate?"

"I think you'll appreciate how we've addressed that." Jennifer pulled up a website on her laptop, then returned to her spot next to the screen. "We found a low cost Software-as-a-Service (SaaS) application that lets everyone track their time online. Before they leave work, they have to ensure all of their time is in the system, and then each team manager approves the time before the next morning."

"No paperwork." Judy raised her right fist in the air, the same way an Olympic runner might as she won a marathon. "It's all online and even imports directly into our payroll system."

Steve rubbed his chin, interested that such an application existed but a little embarrassed he hadn't found it himself.

Sam sat up. "And it's very easy to use. The employees love it, much better than the paper weekly timesheet."

"The process is really quite simple." Jennifer must have felt a need to explain a little further as she drew a quick diagram of the flow of information. "After each manager approves the time, Judy pulls it into a spreadsheet and then updates our daily report. Then she emails it out to the managers so they can use it to improve on each project. In fact, we have yesterday's completed so we can cover it today."

Steve felt like a parent, aware that everyone was eager for his approval. They deserved it. "Wow, I'm amazed at the progress that's been made."

Steve placed his right down on the firm, strong conference table. "Let's look at this report and see if I can understand it." Although he said it like he was joking, Steve was actually concerned that Jennifer's grasp of numbers would leave him in the dust.

"Judy, why don't you go ahead and hand out the paper copy to everyone?" Jennifer walked to her computer. "I'll put it up on the screen as well. Please note that this is very detailed information for the managers."

Bolty Daily IMPACT Indicators

Project Name	Estimated Hours	Prior Hours Incurred	Today's Hours Incurred	Hours to Complete	% to Comp
GHAI-WASHMA-1	183	83	17	83	45.5%
ADKC-VACUUM-1	2,333	333	37	1,963	84.1%
DDAE-SMARTP-1	1,333	167	17	1,150	86.3%
ENTI-CARALT-1	3,667	733	67	2,867	78.2%
DDAE-MEDDEV-1	2,167	1,333	50	783	36.2%
DJKI-VIDGAM-1	1,792	333	42	1,417	79.1%
TEDE-VIDGAM-1	4,667	833	67	3,767	80.7%
TDMI-MEDDEV-1	2,333	0	0	2,333	100.0%
TDMI-HDTVCO-1	433	0	0	433	100.0%
LNCL-DISHWA-1	4,667	0	0	4,667	100.0%
TOTALS		**3,817**	**295**	**19,463**	**82.6%**

Steve was initially overwhelmed, not knowing where to look or how to interpret the myriad of rows, columns, and numbers.

"Let me show you how this works." Jennifer directed the red laser point to the 'GHAI' project at the top of the list. "Let's look at the first project on the list, the one that starts with GHAI?"

Everyone in the room followed the red dot as Jennifer explained how to read the information and what they could learn from it.

When she finished talking, Sam was on the edge of his seat, still stroking his red beard. "I've always felt lost regarding where we stand with each project each day. I've never known if were hitting the budgeted hours we estimated, and it's always been hard for me to determine if I was doing everything I could to make the projects financially successful."

Steve put his palms down on the table and then moved them from side to side, like he was spreading sand over the surface. "And I've been concerned for a long time that when we have less work we just spread it out among our staff and accept a slower pace until the work picks up again. I think this report will help us manage our best and most expensive resource, our people, better than we ever have."

The next thirty seconds were silent as all five managers, Judy, Jennifer, and Steve mentally interpreted the information. The managers began to discuss problems and trends, and they quickly were figuring out how to improve each project without sacrificing the quality of the deliverable expected by the customer.

Jennifer interrupted the discussion. "Let's go ahead and end this meeting so that everyone can get back to work. We'll keep going with the daily process of updating this report and then reconvene in a couple of weeks when we have a little more experience with it. At that point, we'll have some trending charts put together to give a better graphical representation of how the jobs are progressing, day-by-day."

Steve stood, shaking hands with each person and thanking them for their desire and efforts to improve the company. As everyone exited the room, Jennifer motioned for Steve to stay. With just Steve and Jennifer remaining, she closed the door to the conference room. "We're not done, Steve. There's more information from this report that will be very helpful to you, but it's for you only, unless you want to share it with others."

IMPACT INSIGHT #34
Employees and managers can benefit as much as entrepreneurs from the clarity the right quantitative data brings.

"Okay." Steve walked back to his chair. "By the way, I'm impressed with how you got everyone on board with this daily reporting. So, what do you have for me?"

"Getting the daily time from the employees allows us, with almost pinpoint accuracy, to know what our gross profit per day is." Jennifer sat in front of her laptop.

Instead of sitting, Steve stood behind the chair, resting his arms on the top of its back, his speech moving a little faster. "If we know our gross profit per day, then we can know a lot of things. Like what's happening with our backlog and if we're operating at, below, or over our break-even point."

"Yes, exactly." Jennifer pulled the following chart up on the screen. "And those are the key ingredients to knowing if we win or lose every day, at least in this business. Here's a representation of what the last several days have looked like in terms of gross profit."

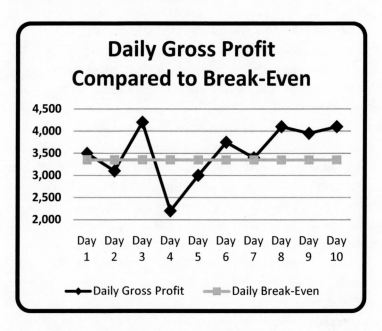

Steve began to point and count out loud. "So, two of the last ten days we lost money, on three of the days we broke even, and on the other five we actually made some money. Is that right?"

Jennifer nodded.

"Are you including my salary in your overhead number? Does it also include the sales team, Judy, and Cindy?" Steve asked.

"Yes. The total overhead is about $3,350 per day. So, day Ten is actually yesterday. Looks like we won yesterday." Jennifer clapped her hands. "Nice!"

"Very nice!" Steve raised both hands over his head and he couldn't stop smiling. "I've always believed that measuring these types of things and holding people accountable to them helps improve overall performance."

"You're exactly right, and this is the information that, when

measured as you described, will have the most impact on the business."
Jennifer took another drink of water. "So we know gross profit and overhead
per day. But we're still missing the third metric for our Daily IMPACT
Indicators--backlog. Once we add that to this daily report, we'll be able to
see the fluctuations in our balance of future work from day-to-day."

Steve nodded his head, his eyes wider than normal. "With that
information I really will know if I win or lose every day."

The two enjoyed a few moments of silence, with Steve marveling at
their progress. Jennifer spoke first. "You know, the interesting thing is that
most business owners and entrepreneurs don't think they can get this
information every day. I think I've heard every excuse in the book as to why
it's not possible. But I've yet to find a company that can't generate this
information if everyone is onboard and willing to make it work."

Jennifer pushed the power button on the projector. The light went out
while the cooling fan kept running. "Back when Bolty was smaller and only
had one or two projects going at a time, you enjoyed clarity by being
involved in every detail, knowing if you were winning or losing each day.
But with all of the employees, projects, and other complexities, you have to
use the right numbers to get the clarity you need about your performance."

"And, of course, they have to meet the IMPACT criteria." Steve
grinned as he reflected on his first meeting with Jennifer. "Jennifer, I was
definitely skeptical when we first met, but now I'm a believer. Every
business needs this kind of information, or they will struggle to be as
competitive as they can. These reports really give us a powerful advantage."

Jennifer closed her laptop, the projector still cooling. "We're ready
to move on to the weekly report. I should have the first draft ready by next
week." Jennifer departed, leaving Steve alone in the large, quiet conference
room.

*Things are really headed in the right direction now. They even seem
to be getting better at home. But I don't have nearly as much clarity with the
family as I do the business. We're spending time together, but what are we
really trying to achieve?* Then Steve had an idea, and he couldn't wait to run
it by Aubrye.

21
METRICS

Just a week and a half later, it was a sunny, warm spring day in Salt Lake City. The grass was turning green and the tulips and fruit trees were in bloom. Steve's family was enjoying a rebirth, as was Bolty in its transition to IMPACT information.

With Aubrye's input, Steve was going to hold a family meeting later that day. He had put a lot of thought into how he could help his family improve, not too much unlike the way he was improving his business. But first he needed to meet with Jennifer to review her progress on Bolty's weekly report. He wasn't completely sold that these reports would improve employee morale and longevity, fixing his problem of employee turnover.

Steve had invested heavily in training and developing his people, and he watched all of those efforts on his two strongest employees walk out the door just a month earlier when they quit. Sure, he would have had to fire two additional people in the layoff if they stayed, but that pain would pale in comparison to the value these programmers brought to the company.

Jennifer sat down in Steve's office and placed a stack of papers on the front of his desk, obviously prepared for their meeting. "Steve, I have a question to start our discussion. But I need to, momentarily, have you imagine you're not sitting in this office. Just for the sake of really understanding what I'm about to ask, imagine you're on a deserted island, stranded and disconnected from communication with anyone or anything, especially with the happenings here at Bolty."

Steve stared at his iPhone on the desk and chuckled like a 20-year prisoner might when he finally was released from captivity into freedom. "Oh, I like the sound of that!" He waggled his eyebrows. "All I need is a drink with an umbrella in it and I'm set."

"Yes, I knew you would enjoy this analogy." Jennifer smiled. "But what if you still needed to run this business from this remote and isolated location?"

"There's no way I could do it." Steve waived his right hand side-to-side, signaling for help. "I've tried going on vacation for a week and I end up on phone calls and responding to emails the whole time I'm gone, and it still takes me a few days to catch up on everything else when I get back. It makes me never want to leave the business for more than a day or two, tops."

Jennifer lifted her thin, brown eyebrows. "So, you're still pretty dependent on being in this office, obtaining qualitative information each day, to know how the business is doing, right?"

Steve looked at the floor while nodding. *Wow, now I see how dependent I really am on being here to run the business. Another thing I didn't do right.* Steve sighed.

Jennifer pulled her hair behind her ears. "Okay, but consider this possibility. Every week a bottle with a message in it floats to the shore of your deserted island. You pull the cork out and unfold a regular-sized piece of paper. The data, which adheres to the IMPACT criteria, on that paper enables you to stay in touch with your business, know what's happening, and, believe it or not, actually make good decisions to improve your company."

Jennifer leaned forward, placed her right index finger on the stack of papers she placed on the desk, and asked, "What would have to be on that piece of paper for it to empower you to accomplish that, to have clarity about your business without being exposed to any qualitative information?"

Steve's mind began to fill with doubt and disbelief. "There's no way a piece of paper could replace being in this office every day. I don't think one page would be near enough, to be honest."

"Steve, I need you to let go of your dependence on qualitative information for just a minute. I know this is difficult for you to see right now, but how do you think large companies run their businesses? How do absentee owners stay on top of their enterprises?"

> **IMPACT INSIGHT #35**
>
> *Most entrepreneurs initially resist the change to less dependence on qualitative data. However, once they do it, they almost always wish they had done it sooner.*

Steve immediately thought of the only absentee business owner he knew. "You know, I have a neighbor, Desmond, who runs a successful business. And he's never there. He's always off gallivanting around the world on some safari or other cool place with his family." Steve reflected on Desmond's tall tales of being chased by lions and scaling the walls of ancient temples in far off, mysterious lands he shared at a recent neighborhood party. "I've wondered how he does that."

Jennifer sat back, seeming to endorse Desmond's lifestyle by the way she smiled. That irritated Steve a little, but he wanted to hear her out. "Without knowing any details, I would guess that he's learned to run his business almost entirely on quantitative data, and most of it comes from one of the six scoreboards we're implementing here at Bolty. Plus, he likely has some very smart, good people working for him who keep things going while he's gone and some bulletproof systems and processes that protect his business model."

"I asked him about that once. He said those three things made it possible--reports, great managers, and systems. I wish I could do what he does."

"Interesting." Jennifer pulled a notepad from her bag and wrote on it for a few moments. "Now, let's change the context from a deserted island to your neighbor's situation. What do you think you would need on a piece of paper every week to be able to do what he's doing?"

Steve had never thought about his business like this. *I don't even know where to begin. But maybe some of what we're already tracking should be on there.* "How about gross profit per week along with our backlog? This is on the daily report, but seeing it weekly would probably be helpful, too."

"Yes, that's a start. But what about everything else?" Jennifer lowered her eyes and touched her cheek, as if she were thinking. "Let me come at this another way. Bolty has several functions to make it go-- marketing, sales, engineering, programming, customer service, human resources, accounting, and finance. To get an accurate weekly summary of Bolty's overall performance, we should have one to three key metrics from each of these areas."

> **IMPACT INSIGHT #36**
> *The most effective weekly business metrics report should include data from every discipline, or department, of the company.*

Steve thought through all of the things that might be included, trying to get ahead of his finance executive just once. "Okay, I think I get it. So what are the areas again?"

"Here, I have them on this paper." Jennifer pushed spreadsheet-like document, categories and numbers, across the desk toward Steve. "I've gone through and tried to identify some of the numbers that seem to be the most critical, and I've pulled data, as best as I could, for each metric so we could see what it looks like and determine its usefulness."

Steve studied the information. He and Jennifer spent the next thirty minutes discussing each department of the business and the pivotal performance drivers in each. They decided on one to three metrics for each of the following departments: marketing & sales, engineering, programming, customer service, and human resources. Then they found eight total critical numbers from accounting and finance. Jennifer quickly filled out her pre-developed weekly IMPACT Indicators spreadsheet and the two sat back and studied the report.

Jennifer pointed at the newly created report on her laptop screen. "I have already reviewed a lot of this with Judy, but I'll make sure she gathers the necessary information to complete this report each week. We'll start with this spreadsheet, but then we'll get it into an even more intellectually accessible format with charts and graphs."

> **IMPACT INSIGHT #37**
> *The most successful entrepreneurs can fit all of the key business metrics they need to run their businesses onto one page.*

Steve continued to study the numbers on the report. "So, I can almost see how this report would help me run the business even if I weren't here, mired in the day-to-day qualitative information. But I'm not planning a three month hiatus to Hawaii or anything like that, yet." Steve smiled, almost hearing ukuleles playing Hawaiian beach music in the background. "But how does this report help me retain my key employees?"

Jennifer folded her arms and concentrated on the report for a few seconds. "Do you remember when we talked about how you would know if you win or lose every day?"

Steve nodded.

"Put yourself in your employees' shoes. How do they know if they win or lose every day or week at their job?"

Steve shifted in his seat. "By how much they help the company be profitable each day?"

Jennifer cringed slightly. *That must have been the wrong answer.* "One trap that some businesses fall into when they try to switch to using quantitative data is that they become solely focused on profit. Now, profit isn't bad unless it's all you focus on. A company has to be profitable if it's going to be able to keep paying its employees and continue fulfilling its mission. But it's only a piece, albeit a significant one, in the overall puzzle."

"Jennifer, hearing this from you is a little surprising, considering your background in finance." Steve liked giving Jennifer a hard time.

Jennifer held up her hands, like a criminal captured in the act of her crime. "I know, sometimes I even get caught in the trap of only chasing profit. But employees won't respond well if all you want them to do is make profit. They want to feel a part of something bigger than themselves, like they're making more than just a contribution to Bolty's pocketbook."

"So, are you talking about sharing profits with employees?"

"Actually, no, although that's an important subject for another day. I'm talking about an organization that is purpose-driven, wherein profit is just a means to accomplishing a greater purpose. And that over-arching purpose is something each employee wants to make a positive contribution to."

Jennifer pointed at the desk calendar facing Steve. "With the daily reporting in place, everyone has a much clearer picture about the contribution they can make to the company. And the weekly reporting will strengthen everyone's ownership of making the company successful. But what is the real motivation for employees to come to work and give their very best every day?"

Steve really wanted to understand where Jennifer was going with this. "Having just survived the layoff, I think the remaining employees are motivated for their paycheck, albeit it's only 90% of what it used to be."

"Sure, everyone needs to get paid, but then why do so many people volunteer their time for free to so many causes. Coaching youth sports teams, helping with political campaigns, and so many other worthwhile charitable, educational, and even professional activities."

Steve raised his hands up, holding his palms open, and widened his eyes. "Whoa, I'm getting lost here."

"I'm sorry, but please just stay with me for a minute." Jennifer lowered her eyebrows, then lifted them, as if an idea had clicked in her head. "I think the reason people give their time away for free is because it's for something they care about, or maybe they are even passionate about. You said you've coached your son in basketball before. Why did you do that for free?"

"Because I wanted to spend time with my son. And I love basketball, and I enjoy teaching others about the game."

"You see, you did it because there was a cause or a purpose for which you carried a passion—your son and basketball." Jennifer's speech accelerated a little, obviously energized by her thoughts and Steve's response. "How do we get employees to feel that way, to have that passion, for what we are trying to accomplish at Bolty? Is this just a job and paycheck, or is there something more to why people want to work here?"

The sick feeling in Steve's stomach came back and he felt like the worst CEO for his business possible. "Jennifer, I don't think anyone here has that kind of passion. At least it hasn't come from me the last several months. I've just been trying to survive, to save this business."

Jennifer's warm smile was full empathy. "Steve, let me tell you what your employees are saying. I won't name names, but just listen to this for a minute."

Jennifer pulled up a document on her laptop and scrolled through a lot of words. "Okay, here it is. I asked some employees about the purpose of Bolty and what they're passionate about. I made my notes in this program as they talked. One employee talked about the cutting edge of technology Bolty is involved with, using it to do more for Bolty's customers. Another talked about enjoying the projects that she gets to work on that are challenging or that give her opportunities to learn new things. Several of the interviewees wanted to know more about what they could do to help Bolty be successful. They enjoy the work they do and find that it's solving real problems for the end consumers of mobile phones, medical devices, and even video games. A different employee said he loves the satisfaction of seeing someone use a product that Bolty helped engineer and design software for. Notice how none of them said anything about a paycheck, and this was right after the layoff."

Steve was surprised at the positive comments. "I guess I've only been seeing the negative side of this business. All of those things are true, and it's why I was passionate to start this business in the first place."

Jennifer's voice slowed. "So, we have this weekly report in hand. This is a scoreboard we can use to judge our performance, and the employees can also be included in understanding how they can positively impact these results we're measuring. That will give them great clarity about what they can specifically do to help the company. And that clarity will help them be greater contributors to the overall purpose of Bolty."

Steve looked at Jennifer and realized that she was exactly like him. An entrepreneur who was passionate about helping other entrepreneurs, just like he was passionate about advancing technology and improving the software used to run electronic-heavy devices. "So I'm still not clear on one thing. Each of the employees has different things they're passionate about. How does that translate into wanting to help Bolty?"

"It's actually okay for everyone's passions to be different. That's normal. But they need to see how Bolty is going to help them achieve their purposes and passions. And there's only one way to do that."

Steve sat up, intrigued. Jennifer stood and walked to Steve's window, then turned back to look at him. Steve could see his favorite majestic mountain range, always so inspirational to him, standing behind Jennifer as if to endorse her next comments. "We have to invest in our people, help them grow and develop by being challenged in their work and expertise, and then they will never want to leave. We measure how Bolty improves because of them, and they get better and more skilled. And they keep coming back for the new challenges and the tangible progress they are a part of here at Bolty."

Steve tried desperately to process what Jennifer was saying. As if she could tell she'd lost him, Jennifer began to explain. "What if I was to tell you that research and studies show that most companies fail to utilize even 50% of their employees' skills, expertise, energy, and potential? Do you think Bolty fits into that category?"

> **IMPACT INSIGHT #38**
> *Many entrepreneurial companies use 50% or less of their employees' skills, experience, and overall abilities to help their businesses.*

"It all depends on what projects we get. We get a lot of mundane work that isn't very challenging. I think we underutilize our programmers a lot of the time, and the engineers for that matter. They end up pushing out project specs and plans for uninspiring and unchallenging work a lot of the time. They usually seem pretty bored, although that's how most engineers look even when they're excited." Steve winked, hoping Jennifer would get his joke. "So how do we get the employees excited about mundane work?"

"I don't know, but I'll bet you can figure it out. But there has to be a way to allow them to use their skills and creativity to standardize some of the more routine systems."

Steve rested the tips of his fingers on his right hand against his chin. "Come to think of it, we do seem to reinvent the same wheel over and over. There's some potential there. With better systems and processes to handle some of their current workload, I could have them spend time improving in some of the new technologies so we can get a leg up on our competition."

"Now you're talking. This will make the company more successful because we'll have a more effective solution for the routine work and off-the-chart competencies in the high-end work, the type of work where no one else can compete with our expertise. And, the margins are always better in the high-end work because we have few, if any, competitors that can keep up with us in that arena."

Steve began to capture a glimpse of what he could really do with his company. *I know this market, and I know where it's going. We can become the leaders in our industry with this focus, instead of just accepting the bid-for-work mentality where you fight against the same three or four competitors for each project.* "Jennifer, I love this direction. This will make Bolty a great company to work for, and, to be honest, this is the most excited I've been about being part of this company than I have in years."

IMPACT INSIGHT #39

The more employees feel the company is accomplishing a greater good, the more they will help the company succeed. And the more they help it succeed, the better the company becomes. They feed one another.

So, the formula is quite simple." Jennifer typed while she talked. "The biggest contribution each employee can make to the company is, ironically, to improve themselves. Bolty can help them improve by giving them opportunities to grow and develop on the job. Then the more they grow and develop, the more they help Bolty be successful. And it continues in this upward spiral, the employees and Bolty each helping each other achieve new levels of success."

Jennifer clasped her hands together, intertwining fingers. "They need to feel like they're getting as much from the relationship as Bolty, and they need to feel like Bolty is accomplishing bigger and more meaningful things than they could on their own or working for someone else."

Steve looked at the digital clock on the wall next to the bookshelf-- 5:14 PM. "Jennifer, I need to go. I'm going to keep thinking about this concept. In fact, it will help me with something I'm doing tonight with my family in about 30 minutes."

He walked to his whiteboard, put an "X" in the box next to 'Key employees left.' "What's next on our list?"

	PROBLEM	SOLUTION
X	Barely made payroll	Monthly IMPACT Indicators
X	Out of cash	Quarterly IMPACT Forecaster
X	Key employees left	Daily/Weekly IMPACT Indicators
	Large customer left	Annual IMPACT Forecaster
	IRS, Lawsuit, Vision for future	5-Year IMPACT Forecaster
	Financial leader deficiencies	IMPACT CFO Services

They both glanced at Steve's whiteboard, and Jennifer pointed to the next empty box. "I'll be working on our one-year forecast, with an emphasis on how to use it to understand how certain events will impact our business in the short to medium-term future. I'll have it ready by this time next week."

Steve remembered arranging a dinner at a local restaurant for that night, hoping to meet her husband and get to know her in a more social setting. He also wanted Aubrye to finally meet the person who had helped him so much with the company. "Great. Are we still on for tonight?"

"Yes, my husband and I are planning on it."

"See you at 7:30." Steve left the building and began the commute. He couldn't stop thinking about his conversation with Jennifer. It opened his mind to a host of opportunities, at work and at home.

22
DESSERT

Using his hands-free earpiece and voice recognition dialer, Steve called his wife during the drive home. The sun had another hour before it would set, and the clear blue sky made Steve feel like anything was within the realm of possibility.

"Hello," he said. Someone answered the phone, but he only heard the rustling of paper and running water for the first five seconds. A little louder this time. "Hello?"

"Hi Daddy." Emma's voice was sweet.

"Emma, can I talk to your mom?"

"Okay, but I'll have to get her from Kingdom Never-ever-land." Emma always had a castle and princess adventure going on in her mind, and sometimes Aubrye played the wicked queen or the fairy princess.

"Hi." Aubrye's voice came through the phone.

Steve laughed. "Sorry to take you away from Never-ever-land. So what character are you playing today?"

Aubrye was breathing hard. "I'm a spy for the King of another land, and Queen Emma has chased me to the waterfall of Hysteria, which is our bathtub."

Steve laughed louder. "I have no idea where she comes up these fantastic stories. I was calling to see if we're still okay for the family meeting when I come home. Is everybody there?"

"Yeah, they're all here. Are you on your way?"

Steve entered the onramp to I-15. "Yep. I'll be there in 20 minutes."

"I'm taking the back seat on this, right? When we talked about your idea I was under the impression you were going to run the show. Am I supposed to play some other role than a participant?"

Steve accelerated as he prepared to merge with the freeway traffic. "No, I'm taking the lead. I've put some serious thought into this. I hope it goes well."

"Me too. See you soon." Aubrye hung up.

Steve finished the drive. He had told the family the night before that they would have a family meeting when he got home from work the next night, and he was anxious to get home and get it started. Steve walked through the empty kitchen to the family room. The tan walls, white trim, and dark brown furniture made it, by far, the nicest room in the house. Of course, the 60 inch plasma HDTV didn't hurt. It was also a reminder they could have saved more money when the business was doing better to help them through the lean times now. Tyler was watching his favorite basketball team, the Utah Jazz.

It's going to be hard to pull him away from that game. "You ready for the family meeting."

"Dad, do we have to do this now? I don't want to miss this game. The Jazz are wiping the floor with your Lakers." Growing up in Southern California, Steve's allegiance to the Los Angeles Lakers was a way of life, although it occupied far less of his thoughts now than in his youth.

"Yes, we need to do this now. This is very important, and I need you to be a part of it." Steve sounded more authoritative than he meant.

"Well, maybe I'm not going to participate until the game is over." Just as Tyler finished, Aubrye and the three girls, Zoe, Stacey, and Emma, joined Steve and Tyler in the family room. Aubrye spoke. "We're all ready."

Tyler sat up and jumped right into the discussion, probably thinking that by speaking first he would gain an advantage. "I'm not participating until after the game is over."

Steve shrugged his shoulders and raised his eyebrows toward his wife, indicating he wasn't sure how to proceed. Then he figured he better take this head-on. "Tyler, I promised to take your mom on a date tonight, and this family meeting needs to happen before we leave."

"How much longer is the game?" Aubrye asked.

"The second quarter is almost over and the Jazz are up by eight. I think they're going to hand a loss to the Lakers tonight." Tyler leaned back into the leather sofa.

Steve felt frustrated. Everyone in the family had been told about this meeting. "How about if I promise we'll be done in time for you to see the second half?"

Tyler clenched his jaw, then asked, "Do I even have a choice? It's not fair. No one else is missing something they'd rather be doing."

Aubrye looked at Steve as though she were silently saying 'this is your battle not mine.' Steve felt impatient and almost snapped on his son, then decided to sweeten the deal. "Tyler, here's my final offer. You can TiVo what you're missing, and you'll get to watch the second half and we'll bring you and everyone else a treat home from the restaurant we're going to. Or," he winked at Tyler, "are you too scared my Lakers are going to bust the Jazz?" Tyler gave a little grin. Steve clapped his hands. "Can we get this meeting started now?"

Tyler nodded and Emma, the seven-year-old, jumped up and down. Tyler used the remote to TiVo the game, then he turned the TV off. Everyone took a seat on one of the two couches that faced each other at a slight angle. Steve, Zoe, and Stacey on one and Aubrye, Tyler, and Emma on the other.

Steve, a little nervous, started speaking in a rather strained voice. He cleared his throat, sat up a little straighter and began again. "I have some things I need to say to this family. I know I've been a lousy father, but hopefully you've seen me try to improve a little the last couple of weeks. I want to apologize, and I hope you'll forgive me."

Steve paused, watching for everyone's reactions, but got none. "I want you all to know that I'm committed to not allowing my job to dominate me like that again because this family is too important to me."

Aubrye raised her hand like a student asking for permission to speak. "I've noticed a big difference. I appreciate you spending more time with us and trying to help around the house. Your 'helpfulness' even got me a new hood."

Tyler, who was staring off into space as though he was not paying attention, began to talk like a mix between a rap artist and a cool surfer. "I'm down with Mom's new hood. That was epic." His three younger sisters always laughed at him when he spoke in this silly voice, and this time was no different.

Steve waited for the laughter to die down, worried his meeting would get off track. "So, I've been thinking a lot about our family. I realized that we don't really have a purpose. What are we trying to accomplish? What value is there to us being together?"

After several seconds of silence, Steve decided to try and give some ideas to spark the discussion. "It seems like sometimes we're just going through the motions. We wake up, rush off to school and work, then rush to ball games and dance recitals, do homework, then go to bed. But what meaning are we getting from it? Why are we doing all of this and where is it taking us? And is that where we really want to go?"

Zoe raised her hand. Steve thought Zoe was the most logical of all his children, although he worried what might happen to that when she became a teenager next year. "Yes Zoe." Steve spoke with a permission-to-speak tone.

Zoe's long blonde hair was pulled back in a French braid, Steve's favorite hair-style for his daughter who'd grown four inches in the last six months. And, of course, her trademark headband was in place. Today's was a teal and brown one bedazzled with lots of sparkly stuff. "You and Mom are always going on about how important the family is. But Mom is the best at it. She takes me to the mall, my friend Penny's house, and swim practice." Zoe ticked off the list with her fingers.

"Yeah, I've unfortunately been the opposite of Mom, and I can sure learn a lot from her. We all can." Steve smiled at Aubrye, hoping she would sense how sincere he really was. "Anyone else?"

"I just want to have fun. No chores, no jobs, just focus on hangin' out." Tyler ran his hands through his long black hair. "We never do anything fun anymore, like the time we went camping in the mountains or the family vacation to Disneyland. We need to do that again. The only funny thing that's happened around here in a long time was seeing Dad sprawled out on mom's hood." Tyler smacked his hand in the air as a pretend high-five to his dad.

Steve shook his head. "I'll never live that down, will I?" Steve gave Tyler a wry smile. "Tyler has a good point, although the chores and work are fun if you make them that way."

Steve looked at Emma, sitting between Aubrye and Tyler. "Emma, what do you think?"

"I think we need dessert every night." Emma beamed with confidence, still in the pink and purple princess dress from her adventure with Aubrye. "And a pony."

Emma's comments drew smiles from her three older siblings. Aubrye came to Steve's rescue. "Emma, that's a great suggestion. But," Aubrye lengthened the word, "I think Daddy wants to talk about more than just dessert and ponies. He wants to talk about helping our family do lots of great things for many years into the future. I think dessert, although not at every meal, will probably be part of that." Emma snuggled close to her mom, leaving Tyler on the far end of the couch. Aubrye looked down at Emma. "But we'll have to talk about that pony idea another time."

After a few more minutes of ideas and suggestions, Steve walked over to Tyler and stood in front of him. "I think everything we're talking about, like having fun together and helping each other, is very good. But I also think those ideas are part of a greater purpose. Tyler, I'm going to use you for an example to explain this."

Tyler threw his hands up in the air. "Why are you always picking on me, Dad?"

Steve patted his son's shoulder. "This isn't a slam on you, dude." Tyler relaxed under his father's hand. "I'm not very proud of this, but I did something that hurt Tyler about a month ago. I was supposed to go driving with him, but I blew it by coming home late from work. He needed that driving time to be able to get his license next week, and I let him down. Hopefully we can make it up before his exam next week." Steve pointed at Tyler. "Tyler, did you feel like I was keeping you from achieving your potential, from accomplishing your goal?"

Tyler dropped his hands. "Yeah, that was totally lame. I might not get my license on my birthday now."

Steve walked back and reclaimed his spot on the couch. "So, I kept Tyler from being all he could be. And that is the opposite of what our purpose should be. Our main reason to be together is to help each other become the best we can be. And, remember, this isn't a one-sided relationship, where Mom and Dad are in charge of helping you kids grow. It works the other way--the kids need to help Mom and Dad, too."

Stacey, the black-haired ten-year-old, had been silent until now. "Dad, I don't know what you're talking about."

Steve stood and walked to the kitchen table where he had set down his laptop bag. He pulled out a small pad of paper, then returned to the family room. "Stacey, I think this will help." Steve held the pad in the air. "I made some notes on here about goals I want to set for myself and keep track of so I can do my part to help each one of you become better."

Aubrye scooted to the edge of her couch, trying to see what Steve wrote. He pulled it to his chest, sat down, and smiled slyly at Aubrye, happy to have the upper hand for once. "So, here is the question I asked myself. What can I do to help each of you? Notice this is not about me, but it's about everyone else in the family."

Aubrye was still trying to see Steve's list, unsuccessfully. "I want to make some suggestions for your list."

Steve grinned, but he would not be derailed from what he was trying to teach. "So, I asked myself an even more specific question--what do I need to do every day to help all of you?" Steve emphasized the word 'day', then put his finger under the words he was about to read next. "I need to keep turning the business off for three hours every night, regardless of how bad things are, and focus on spending time with all of you. Family dinner, ball games, recitals, homework, driving lessons, hanging out, whatever."

Aubrye pulled her long, dark, curly hair back. "I think this will make a big difference. Have you kids liked having your dad around more the last couple of weeks?"

Each of the kids nodded, and Steve became a little more confident. "So then I asked myself the same question, but directed toward the things I might do every week." This time Steve emphasized the word 'week'. "I came up with two. First, a date-night with Mom, and, second, help organize a family activity each week, like go to a movie, or something else that would be fun."

"Or maybe a Jazz game every week," Tyler said with more enthusiasm than Steve thought possible in a family meeting that Tyler would likely describe as 'boring'.

Steve smiled. "Probably not every week, but we'll find something fun. So, who thinks they can guess the next question I asked myself?"

Zoe raised her hand, then inflected her voice like at the end of a question. "Monthly?"

Steve gave Zoe a 'thumbs-up' sign. "Bingo. Every month I'll

organize a meeting like this where we can talk about how we're all doing on helping each other. We'll talk about our progress as a family, and we'll figure out how to make it not boring."

Tyler clapped his hands. "So I bet yearly is next."

"Not quite, but close." Steve moved his finger to the next section on the pad. "Every three months, or every quarter, I will help plan and organize a family weekend getaway, like a camping or skiing trip, and I will also put together a family work project, like paint that eyesore for a backyard fence."

Emma stood up straight, as if announcing the arrival of one of her pretend royal friends. "I like quarters." Everyone laughed while Tyler explained what a quarter was in this case.

Then Tyler remembered what his dad actually said. He sighed. "Wait a minute. What's up with this work stuff? I thought we were only doing fun stuff."

"Work is a big part of helping each other Tyler, so we need to do some work. Life is not all play. Besides, we usually have fun when we do work projects together. Like remember when we planted those trees for Mother's Day last year? That was one of the worst mud fights I've ever been in, hands down."

Steve looked back at his list. "Oh, and I almost forgot my favorite thing on here. Every year I will help plan a vacation for the entire family." Steve handed his list to Aubrye, wondering if she was still interested to read it now that he had announced its contents. "That's my list. What do you think?"

Aubrye's mouth was open. The three oldest kids began to suggest exotic and exciting places to go on vacation. But Emma was frowning. Steve looked at his seven-year-old. "What's the matter?"

"There was nothing in there about dessert."

Everyone laughed, including Emma once she realized she'd said something funny. "How about we put you in charge of that, with Mom's help?"

Steve walked back to the kitchen table and put his pad of paper back into his bag. As he returned, he felt empowered by what he perceived to be a very productive meeting. "And here's the amazing part of all of this. The more I focus on helping each of you improve, the better our family will get, and the more we'll all want to be a part of it and help it improve even more."

Steve sat back down in his spot on the couch with Zoe and Stacey. "So, I want to ask all of you to do the same thing I did--create your own list of things you can do to help others in the family. Let's have another family meeting in a month, and we can discuss what you all come up with and we can track the progress I'm making on my list. Any questions about the assignment?"

Steve noticed Tyler glance at his watch. "We're wrapping up here. You'll be back to your game in no time."

"Yeah, but I'll bet the Jazz are really putting the hurt on your Lakers right now. Maybe they won't even come out for the second half." Tyler prodded his father for some good old-fashioned smack-talk. Steve couldn't resist.

"The Lakers' strategy is to let your Jazz run around and wear themselves out in the first half. The Lakers will own the second half." As Steve finished his comment, he mused at how he and his son could banter about a game they weren't even watching.

Aubrye waived her arms, getting the attention of Steve. "So, are we done?"

"Okay, don't forget your homework is due at our next meeting." Steve held his list up. "Meeting adjourned."

Tyler broke for the TV remote and had the game on in seconds, just in time to see the highlights from the first half. Aubrye began to give instructions to Zoe on her babysitting tasks since Tyler was leaving later to go to a friend's house. Steve helped the two youngest girls upstairs and into their pajamas.

With everybody situated and in place, Steve and Aubrye pulled out of the driveway in Aubrye's SUV. "I told you," Steve said, "I haven't driven it since you got the new hood. I wanted to give it a try."

"So, how did you come up with this idea for the family meeting tonight, anyway? That was quite a list, by the way."

Steve took a deep breath. "Somewhere along the line I lost my purpose for the business. We made some good money, but I had lost my passion for making Bolty, and its employees, everything they could be. When the company began to de-rail with the economy, it basically magnified the real problem--I had lost my purpose." The reflection of the street lights on the new, polished hood was clearer than he remembered when they bought Aubrye's SUV a few years earlier. "When I started Bolty I was focused on changing the world with my programming and technology services. But then I became more concerned with losing everything. I forgot why I was even in business. The same thing happened with our family, and it was my fault."

Aubrye adjusted the vent so it would point directly at her. "How did the same thing happen with the family?"

"I was so concerned with losing you, I convinced myself that I had to save the business to not lose you. I know now that wasn't logical, but it was my reality at the time."

Aubrye reclined her seat a little more. "Interesting." She reached over and placed her hand on Steve's arm, which he was resting on the console between the two front seats.

"You and the kids are my most important priority, and the business is a close second. It's how we survive financially and it's a big part of who I am. And, the changes we're making at work are having an impact on how I approach my family life, albeit they are two totally different things."

IMPACT INSIGHT #40
Every entrepreneur has something more important to him than his business. For Steve, it's his family. What is it for you?

Aubrye moved her hand down Steve's arm and grabbed his hand, holding it tightly, giving Steve a warm sensation he hadn't felt in a while. Steve held her hand like he never wanted to let go. Aubrye smiled. "For what it's worth, I like this new-found purpose-driven you."

The two were silent for several minutes, and Steve wished it could continue longer. Aubrye looked at him. "Who are we meeting for dinner again?"

Steve stopped at a red light at a busy intersection. "Jennifer Silverstone and her husband--I don't even know his first name. You remember, she's the financial consultant I told you about. The one that has come in and helped me get the business turned around."

"That's right, sorry I forgot. She's the one you mentioned, that helped you with the layoff, the bank, and all the reports and stuff, right? I'm looking forward to meeting her."

Steve pulled into a large parking lot. The restaurant was obviously busy, so they had to park a long distance from the building.

"That looks like Jennifer and her husband over there." Steve pointed to a couple getting out of a car just a couple of stalls over.

Jennifer and a dark-haired man walked toward Steve and Aubrye. As they got closer, Steve felt shorter and shorter. Jennifer's husband looked like he could play tight end for the New York Jets. He had to be at least six foot six inches tall, very muscular, and strong facial features that would intimidate defending linebackers.

Jennifer waived. "Hi, Steve. This is my husband, Trent." Steve and Trent shook hands.

Steve clicked his keychain remote to lock the doors, a quiet chirp sounding with a brief flash of the headlights. "This is my wife, Aubrye. Aubrye, this is Jennifer, and her husband, Trent."

Jennifer extended her hand and shook Aubrye's. "I sure enjoy working with your husband."

Aubrye nodded. "He's said wonderful things about the difference you've made at the business. Thank you."

Jennifer almost blushed, clearly uncomfortable with public praise. "It's been my pleasure."

"Well, we both had to park a mile away," Steve said. "Let's go see if they still have our reservation."

The two couples enjoyed their evening getting to know one another, and Steve even remembered to order extra desserts to bring home for the kids. With things becoming more and more clear, Steve was gaining confidence. But he was still a little afraid of the future. *Will I really be able to turn Bolty around and get it all the way back on track? Will my efforts with the family work?*

23
PROJECTIONS

Just one week, later Steve sat in the waiting area of the local DMV while Tyler took his driving test. Steve and Tyler finished the required driving hours the night before and, although the wary father hated to admit it, Tyler was becoming a pretty good driver. It appeared as though Tyler would get his license on his birthday after all.

The old brick state-run facility was busier than Steve thought for 9 o'clock on a Friday morning. Steve was glad he didn't have to wait in any of the long, winding lines of people, and he was especially grateful he was not related to the small child throwing an echoing temper tantrum at the far end of the building.

So much for coming early to beat the crowds. He was anxious to hear the results of the test, hoping it would work out as Tyler wanted. *What an interesting parallel to Bolty. I felt a tremendous amount of apprehension and fear when I couldn't figure out what was going to happen. Clarity seems to effectively dispel all of that. But why do I still feel nervous about the future of Bolty? That's right; we still haven't done the Annual and 5-Year IMPACT Forecaster. And I still need to get used to processing the data to make strategic decisions. There's no way I could run my business without being there every day, like my neighbor Desmond, the world-traveling neighbor. But maybe someday.*

Steve looked up and saw Tyler, beaming his trademark smile with a dimple in his right cheek, black straggly hair in his face. The newly licensed driver held two thumbs up as he approached, probably breaking a speed-walking record in the process. "I did it, Dad."

The two exchanged a high five. "Congrats, son. I knew you could."

Tyler completed the necessary paperwork, but Steve could tell the teenager was aching to get out on the road. "That's some pretty long hair in this photo."

Tyler grabbed the license from his dad. With obvious nervous nonchalance, Tyler put the license in his wallet, stuffed the wallet in his back pocket, and walked out of the building like he was carrying the MVP trophy from the state basketball tournament. Steve felt the joy that always came when his children excelled or accomplished something worthwhile.

Steve searched for his keys as they walked to his car, then realized Tyler had them. "I need to get to work now. Do you want me to drop you off at school?"

"Not really." Tyler flipped his long black hair to the side, squinting a little as he looked into the sun. "I'd rather go catch a movie, or maybe hang at the skate park."

"Ha ha, smart guy." Steve smiled. "Yeah, those sound like attractive options. But you'll have your fun tonight when you get to watch your favorite basketball team from the front row."

"No doubt, those are some phat tickets. Thanks again for hooking me up." Tyler held out his fist, and Steve bumped it with his own.

"You're welcome. Now let's get you to school so I can get to my meeting on time." Steve pointed at the keys in Tyler's hand. "You've got the keys, so it looks like you're driving."

Landscapers were mowing the grass and tending to the flowers in front of Alta High, but there wasn't a student in sight. "Weird how quiet this place is when everyone's in class." Tyler stopped next to the landscapers' trailer. "Thanks again for taking me, Dad."

"You're welcome. Now get to class, you licensed sixteen-year-old. And text Mom. She'll be excited for you." Steve moved to the driver's seat and headed to the office, thinking about the connection between clarity and anxiety.

Steve walked in his office to find Jennifer sitting in her usual spot working on her iPad. "Sorry I'm a couple of minutes late. I took Tyler to his driving test and it was a little busier than I expected."

When Jennifer finished typing and set her trendy tech device on the chair next to her, she turned toward Steve, raising one eyebrow. "Did he pass?"

Steve nodded. "Yep. So let this be your fair warning. Drive with caution, and pedestrians better stay off the sidewalks." Steve could feel his face almost crack with the proud smile he knew he had on his face. "By the way, he'll be driving a car that's almost as old as him, a small rusty red Toyota pickup truck with about 150,000 miles on it. Just wanted you to know."

The two chuckled. Steve pulled his laptop from his bag, placed it in its usual spot on the desk, and plopped into his overstuffed black leather executive chair. "That DMV got me thinking about something I wanted to run by you."

"What is it?" Jennifer folded her hands, her usual position when he knew she'd be listening to him.

"Well, I think I started to see how anxiety and clarity work. They're negatively correlated, meaning the more you have of one, the less you usually have of the other. Is that right?"

Jennifer nodded her head. "That's usually how it works. When we first met, I'd say your anxiety and fear was high and your clarity was very low. Would you agree?"

IMPACT INSIGHT #41
Fear and anxiety are negatively correlated to clarity. The more clarity an entrepreneur has, the less fear and anxiety he will feel.

Steve wrinkled his nose and spoke with a little bit of pain in his voice. "Yes, I would absolutely agree. But I still feel some of it. It's not gone." Steve winced. "You'd think with all of the changes I've made, I'd feel great 24/7."

"No, not at all." Jennifer crossed her legs. "There are two reasons for that, and the first is that you can never get rid of anxiety completely.

Business is risky, and, as you know, certainly not for the faint of heart. Competitors are always trying to get you, and you'll always worry a little about keeping your customers satisfied. But that feeling of anxiety and fear can be minimized."

Jennifer moved to Steve's whiteboard and found a black marker. "The second reason is that we still haven't gotten as much clarity as we need, especially about the future." Pointing to the list on the board, the CFO consultant said, "We still have a few more things to put in place before we're doing everything we can to understand where we've been, where we're at now, and where we're going."

PROBLEM	SOLUTION
[X] Barely made payroll	Monthly IMPACT Indicators
[X] Out of cash	Quarterly IMPACT Forecaster
[X] Key employees left	Daily/Weekly IMPACT Indicators
[ ] Large customer left	Annual IMPACT Forecaster
[ ] IRS, Lawsuit, Vision for future	5-Year IMPACT Forecaster
[ ] Financial leader deficiencies	IMPACT CFO Services

"I got it." Steve eyed the list. Those last three boxes unchecked were bugging him, and he wasn't sure if he could whip up more enthusiasm to tackle more new information. That familiar 'what's going to happen?' feeling welled into his gut again. "Wasn't our meeting this morning supposed to be about the annual forecast?"

Jennifer put the marker down and returned to her chair. "Yes, and I also have the first draft of the five-year model ready for your review as well. Forecasting is not always an entrepreneur's favorite activity, but it's always worthwhile."

Steve placed his right fist in his left hand, both elbows on the arm rests of his chair. "I'm curious to see how this creates clarity. When I think about the future, I can't see much beyond next week, let alone an entire year. It feels like a wild guess to me."

Jennifer tilted her iPad into an almost vertical position so Steve could see the annual forecast on the colorful screen. Jennifer explained how she came up with each of the numbers, detailing her assumptions and other evidence used in the process. Steve was amazed how much more thorough and calculated her approach was when compared to his prior feeble efforts to plan for a year into the future.

Steve grimaced, still skeptical. "I'm still not sure how much I can trust this. This plan is saying we'll have 9% growth this year. But so many things could cause that plan to derail."

Jennifer lowered the iPad, laying it on the desk. "Sure, but so many things could happen to actually make us have better than 9% growth, too."

Still grimacing, Steve shrugged his shoulders. "I see your point. But what's the point of planning when a change in just one of so many variables can throw everything off?"

"Steve, let me mention two of more than a dozen ways projections empower you." Jennifer held up one finger. "Creating a plan gives you something to compare to your actual performance. This is often referred to as variance analysis, and it's very helpful to really understand all of the critical drives of Bolty's performance."

A loud bang came from next door, the first of the morning. Jennifer didn't even flinch. *She must be getting used to working here.* "In fact, I have yet to see a company stick to a monthly diet of comparing budgets to actual performance and not learn a lot more about their business model than they thought possible, and usually a lot more about it than most of their competitors."

> **IMPACT INSIGHT #42**
> *Planning for the future and then tracking performance against that plan will help entrepreneurs gain competitive advantages.*

Steve folded his arms, stretching his back. "I've never done that, but I can see how that would be helpful."

"And here is just one example. A company in an industry devastated by a tough economy applied these principles to their business. The result is that they have been able to navigate through the landmine of which many of their competitors have become casualties. They were able to quickly fix and correct their problems, and they proactively adjusted their business to be able to survive the downturn. They'll tell you that comparing their results to their plans each month is 100% the reason they're still in business."

Steve's eyes widened, feeling some empathy for this other company's plight. "Wow, that's a powerful testimonial."

Holding up a second finger, Jennifer said, "If that's not reason enough, then consider this second benefit. With a plan in place, you can quickly adapt if your actual performance deviates very far from your plan. For example, last year one of my customers beat its budgeted revenue by more than 20% the very first month of the year. The next month was almost as far ahead of schedule. Rather than blindly hope their business would have enough cash and resources to handle the growth, they had clear, actionable data in front of them, they quickly made the changes required to take their expected growth in stride, remaining competitive and viable."

Arms still folded, Steve bowed his head forward. "Seems like we could have benefitted from that same information last year, too."

Jennifer walked back to the white board, underlining 'Large customer left'. "What were your concerns when you found out you were losing that customer?"

Steve unfolded his arms while swiveling his chair to face the whiteboard. "I was scared. I wasn't sure how badly it would hurt us, or if it might even put us out of business." Steve crossed his legs. "Just like the line at the DMV, I had little clarity, meaning I had a lot of fear and anxiety."

Jennifer underlined 'Annual IMPACT Forecaster'. "And the way to quickly gain clarity in that situation is to pull that customer out of your annual budget and see where that leaves you. I did that, and we're still going to grow 9% this year, if everything comes together based on our reasonable assumptions. All that worry is eliminated."

Steve looked out his window. The sky was clear, affording a picturesque view of the mountain range he so admired. "This is great information. I can't believe the progress we've made in just a couple of months." Steve allowed himself a shy smile. "I guess I can take it easy on the antacids. I feel so great now, maybe I can start eating spicy food again."

"Well, I don't think we're quite there yet. We still have some progress to make." Jennifer underlined the next group of problems 'IRS, Lawsuit, Vision for future'. "Based on our conversations and the understanding I have gained regarding Bolty's structure and operations, I have prepared a 5-Year IMPACT Forecaster, or model, that allows us to see where we are headed from a very big-picture perspective."

"Whoa." Steve held up his hand like a police officer directing traffic. "Projecting one year into the future seems like a real 'crystal ball' effort to me. Five years is impossible."

"Almost impossible." Jennifer returned to her chair again. "But we have a very real bill from the IRS we need to pay. They charge inordinately expensive interest and penalties, and we need to figure out how to structure our payments to them so we can make them go away as quickly as possible without starving the business of the cash flow it needs to survive and grow."

Steve flashed back six months earlier to the day the IRS auditor visited, and the subsequent weeks of communication thereafter, resulting in some of the worst news he could have ever received. Comments like 'misclassifying employees' and 'years worth of payroll taxes' kept cropping up when he spoke to one IRS agent or another, and he'd felt trapped and angry. How could he owe them so much money? "Oh, I hate even thinking about that issue."

"I know." Jennifer nodded empathetically. *She must have other customers who have had similar problems. Maybe I'm not the only guy struggling to survive that got caught in the tax Gestapo's crosshairs.* "I've added it to our five-year plan to see what our best options are to handle it. And I've added some different scenarios surrounding how we should manage the lawsuit as well."

Jennifer flipped to a worksheet named 'legal costs' and pointed to some cost projections and other assumptions. "The attorney firm was very helpful in estimating the defense costs along with a few strategies that could help us decide how to best handle the case. Let me show you how all of this works and how it will help us make the best decisions on these and other strategic items."

Steve and Jennifer spent the next fifteen minutes talking through and running what/if scenarios, such as the cost to try and settle early versus seeing the case all the way through to trial. They modeled all of the major long-term issues to which Steve felt enslaved, and they even talked about a couple of long-term strategies Steve thought might help the business grow and become more profitable. They evaluated the financial ramifications of a profit sharing program to his top employees, something Steve felt he needed to do, especially after they endured a salary reduction. "This is a great tool. I love it. I can see how this will increase my clarity even more and help me make more informed, better decisions."

> **IMPACT INSIGHT #43**
> *Financial Modeling is not pretending to have a crystal ball for the future. It is about understanding the impact certain decisions will have on the future as well as helping the company chart the best course possible in its strategic and tactical initiatives.*

"Good." Jennifer gave the whiteboard a 'we're almost done with this list' look.

Steve took a turn walking to the whiteboard and, using some real flair, wrote an 'X' next to each of the two tasks completed that day. But one still remained. "So, what about this last one? How does this work?"

	PROBLEM	**SOLUTION**
X	Barely made payroll	Monthly IMPACT Indicators
X	Out of cash	Quarterly IMPACT Forecaster
X	Key employees left	Daily/Weekly IMPACT Indicators
X	Large customer left	Annual IMPACT Forecaster
X	IRS, Lawsuit, Vision for future	5-Year IMPACT Forecaster
	Financial leader deficiencies	IMPACT CFO Services

Steve returned to his chair as Jennifer began to speak. "We've put a lot of tools in place, and Judy and the rest of the team are going to need some ongoing help and leadership to keep these things working and relevant. Many businesses don't have a full-time CFO, mainly because they don't need one. But they can get a lot of value from having someone involved on a part-time basis that knows the business and its employees. It's someone with business, finance, accounting, tax, and general executive management and leadership perspective."

Steve examined the value Jennifer had brought his business. *I might be out of business right now if it weren't for her.* "Can you give me some examples of what that person will do?"

"Sure. They'll meet with you regularly and become an advisor that you'll hopefully involve in most of your major business decisions. They should direct the production of your six scoreboards, ensure they meet the IMPACT criteria, and analyze them regularly and give you and your team comments on performance. They should meet with you monthly at a minimum to review your scoreboards. Your CFO will manage your relationship with the bank and coordinate with your tax CPA and other professionals helping you with compliance and other personal planning issues. Ultimately, this person should take the role of strategic implementer, helping you convert your strategies into actionable tactics that get done. And so much more."

Jennifer is already doing all of that for me. I'd like to have her take this role in my company. I wonder if she's even interested. Bolty's pretty small potatoes compared to some of the other companies she's worked for. With her expertise she could probably work for anybody she wanted to.

Jennifer raised her hands, palms up, shoulder height. "Really, it's everything that a Chief Financial Officer does in a big company, but on a much more flexible and affordable budget than hiring a full-time CFO. If you still want me around, then I'd be very interested in doing that for you. I've really grown to enjoy working with the team here at Bolty, and I'm excited about the future."

Ah, maybe Bolty's not too Podunk after all. Yes! "I was wondering what would happen to you after we got all of this in place. I'd love to have you stay in this part-time, or outsourced, CFO role. You've been functioning as that for the last couple of months anyway."

155

Steve and Jennifer discussed a few specifics of what their relationship would look like moving forward, including costs, which Steve especially appreciated. "Not only are the fees reasonable, but I have a fixed cost that I can plan on. And I don't feel like your billing clock is ticking when I need your help." Steve stood and reached out his hand. "I'm looking forward to a long-term relationship."

IMPACT INSIGHT #44
The most valuable thing a part-time CFO gains while helping to establish the six scoreboards is knowledge about how the business works and what makes it successful. This is wasted if the entrepreneur does not continue to have that CFO be part of his executive team on an ongoing basis.

"Me, too." Jennifer shook his hand. "Thanks for the opportunity to work with you and the rest of your team."

Steve felt a freedom he hadn't experienced in a long time. In fact, it was probably similar to the way Tyler would feel when he finally drove by himself for the first time after school. *Driving is a big responsibility, and I hope Tyler takes it seriously, or he could hurt himself or others. I hope I've got this business to a point where I don't have to hurt my employees or family ever again.*

24
EVOLUTION

Eight months later, in the middle of one of the coldest Januarys in the history of Salt Lake City, Steve sat inside a 737 jet about to take off from the airport. Large flakes of snow had begun to fall, although the storm was new enough that they were immediately melting, making the tarmac wet.

Tyler was next to Steve in the window seat, with Aubrye, seven-year-old Emma, and a much more grown up ten-year-old Stacey across the aisle from him. Zoe, almost thirteen, was proud to sit one row ahead. Just two hours after take-off, the plane would land in San Diego, California, the family's destination for their first annual vacation, planned almost entirely by Steve on an economical budget.

Aubrye smiled, reached across the aisle, and grabbed Steve's hand, squeezing it. He returned the squeeze, then noticed the storm outside the window on her side of the plane had intensified to the point he could not see the terminal. "I can't think of a better time to leave on vacation than this."

The plane finished its taxi and hurtled down the runway, lifting off with speed and ease. Cutting through the unrelenting storm, the snowflakes were a beautiful blur of white. Within minutes, the plane broke through the dark clouds responsible for the tempests, revealing the brilliant sun and a wide expanse of blue sky.

The change in environment was so drastic, Tyler pulled out his ear buds from his iPod and blurted, "Whoa! That's awesome."

With each family member settled into a book or some electronic device to entertain them for the ride, Steve reflected on his journey over the last months. *That was where I was a year ago, in that storm with almost zero visibility. Those were dark days, and I definitely prefer where I am now.*

With the company back on track and making solid progress, earlier that week Steve returned all of the employees at Bolty back to their salaries of almost a year earlier. He even handed out bonuses, making up about 15% of their lost wages from the reduction period. He planned to make all of the lost wages up to them within the next twelve months, and he showed them the details of what the company, and each of them, would need to accomplish to make that happen.

Jennifer and the IMPACT reports were a big part of the turnaround, especially in helping him make the best decisions possible and set a clear strategic course for the company. And Jennifer fit nicely into the role of Bolty's part-time CFO, adding so much value to the company. Steve couldn't imagine running the business without her.

Steve was energized again, just like the early days when he was getting Bolty off the ground. Even though the economy was still struggling, the firm was gaining momentum with its customers and prospects.

As the plane touched down on the beautiful 65 degree day in the lush coastal city, Steve was sad the ride ended. *That was a very pleasant stroll down memory lane.*

Aubrye looked over at him. "Well, I guess the trip is about to begin."

That's right. The journey is just beginning. There's more clarity on the horizon, and I'm headed exactly for where I want to end up.

Concepts

25
IMPACT ACRONYM

Jennifer only briefly explained to Steve the meaning of the each letter in the IMPACT acronym. I have found very few small to medium-sized businesses that have access to reports and quantitative data that meet the standards of all six IMPACT criteria, meaning they are missing out on possible competitive advantages and opportunities to more effectively accomplish their objectives.

You will find more detail below about what each letter of the acronym represents. Each element of the acronym also has at least one real-life example from various entrepreneurial companies, with names and other details either withheld or changed to protect confidentiality.

I-Insightful

You will reach the pinnacle of insightful indicators and information when they foster contemplation and discussion, both strategically and tactically, that actually improves performance. The data and information reported regularly in a business needs to be analyzed and presented in a way that generates independent and creative thought and insight, and the company needs to create forums and opportunities wherein these thoughts and insights can be discussed, allowing the company to capitalize on them.

A few years ago I began working with a company that was receiving financial statements every month, but the entrepreneur was taking ten seconds to look at the bottom-line of the profit and loss statement, making sure it was positive, and then put them in a neat folder in his filing cabinet. He spent no time or mental bandwidth on any other part of his financial statements.

He didn't know what to look for on his monthly reports and didn't understand what they were saying, anyway. He was gleaning no insights about how to improve his business from his data. With some work and training, he now receives, a monthly reporting package with CFO-level analysis that immediately fosters strategic thought and insight, and his business has grown by leaps and bounds as a result, with several impressive awards and recognitions to show for it.

M-Meaningful

What are the most meaningful things that happen in your business? Every business has pivotal performance drivers that ultimately determine its success or failure. These need to be included and highlighted in the reporting functions of the company. Every employee should understand their potential impact on these key drivers, and the indicators of the business should help each employee know what they can do to improve.

A large service provider was not getting data that focused on the pivotal performance drivers that collectively determine the overall success of the company. They needed to drill in on gross profit per customer, billable hours, capacity, and break-even. Within weeks, I helped them illuminate and begin reporting these critical factors. There sales are up 100% over last year, and their profit is growing even faster than that.

P-Precise

You need to be able to trust that the information you receive is accurate. If you find one flaw in the data, then the credibility of all of the data is lost and decision-making becomes fuzzy. Precise also implies the reports are showing the true performance of the company, one without wide variations from month-to-month in gross margin or that fails to implement accrual and sometimes even Generally Accepted Accounting Principles (GAAP) procedures to give the most accurate picture of actual performance, unimpeded by cash basis or other non-standard accounting and finance practices.

I could share so many examples with you of companies that struggle with accuracy, but for the purposes of this book I will limit it to just one. With lots of customers and products, this particular company's gross margin fluctuated from between positive 60% and negative 30% each month. Utilizing a mix of cash and accrual accounting principles, the company lacked quantitative data that was precise. Once the right revenue recognition procedure was implemented, the variance in gross margin from month-to month dropped to less than 3%, which helped them know their gross margin exactly and, more importantly, improve the way they run their business. The result, after several years, is that they have been able to survive in a very tough industry where 75% of their competition has gone out of business. They are profitable and have a bright future.

A-Accessible
The indicators and forecasts need to be easily accessible both intellectually and physically. Intellectual accessibility refers to avoiding large tables of overwhelming data points and, instead, using charts and graphs as much as possible. Physical accessibility is about making the information as easy to access as possible. Forcing people to have a certain kind of software or another user name and password just to access the information creates barriers instead of easy access. Most will not open the attachment to the email you send or they will forget where they saved the document. Print it, distribute it, put it up on the wall, and do anything else required to remove barriers to physical access.

Not too long ago a company asked me to help them put a financial plan together for their future. They were making significant changes to their business model and adding several complex products and financing options to their customers. The 5-Year IMPACT Forecaster™ I created had several pages of assumptions and other detail, not to mention month-by-month and year-by-year summaries and analysis that consisted of thousands of columns and rows of data. Needless to say, this report was not intellectually accessible in its raw form, requiring hours of analysis from even a trained eye to gain the insights the company needed related to cash flow and future profitability. With a few simple charts and graphs embedded into the main assumption pages, I made the projection intellectually accessible, allowing the principals to change assumptions and within seconds understand the impact on their plans. They are now on track to beat their performance from prior years with a more scalable business model.

163

C-Comparative

Numbers and data are meaningless without understanding the context in which they are derived. How did the company do last month, last year, and several years ago? Which direction is it trending? How does the company's performance compare to its industry? These and other questions should be answered by the company's reporting processes.

Several years ago a sales and installation company needed help with receiving and understanding their financial information on a regular basis. One of their greatest deficiencies was they failed to put their performance into context with their historical data as well as with others in their industry. The insights that came from doing this helped them make changes to their staffing and compensation programs that have positively impacted the employees and the company. They have grown consistently since then, and the owners are reaping significant rewards.

T-Timely

Information is only valuable if it can facilitate the development and implementation of strategic and tactical initiatives. The more out-of-date or after-the-fact the information is, the less actionable it becomes.

A few years ago I was introduced to an entrepreneur who claimed it was impossible for his company to generate monthly financial reports until 45 days after the end of the month. I was intrigued to learn what made this small business so much more complex than large multi-national corporations that can generate their monthly information within 15 to 20 days of the month-end. We quickly helped them improve their monthly closing more than 30 days to about the 12th of the following month, and their decision-making has become timelier, too. They continue to grow and have expanded their operations into a large, state-of-the-art facility.

You will learn more about how the IMPACT criteria apply to each kind of scoreboard and your entire accounting and finance function in Chapters 29 to 31.

26
NEED FOR DATA

In chapter nine, Steve and Jennifer have a discussion about an entrepreneur's gut, or intuition, and how it is originally fed by qualitative and anecdotal information. There is nothing wrong with this, especially for a start-up trying to conserve cash and 'bootstrap' its way to paying customers and a solid revenue stream.

As a business grows, however, it inherently becomes more complex. More customers reduce the number of interactions an entrepreneur can have with each one, if any interactions are even possible at all. It usually becomes necessary to hire more employees to take care of the growing list of customers, which makes it more difficult to be intimately involved with the work done by the employees. More customers also usually translates into a need for more suppliers and vendors, requiring an entrepreneur to keep up with all of them as well.

So, by delegating, entrepreneurs solve the problem of becoming disconnected from all of the details as the company grows. But they often fail to put the right quantitative measurement programs in place that sufficiently replace their first-hand knowledge of the happenings and performance of the company. This creates two problems, reliance on qualitative information and lack of clarity.

The entrepreneur still knows some of the customers, and some of them may even call him directly if they have an issue or need to discuss something. If they report a problem, then the entrepreneur begins to think all of the customers have the same problem, even though that one customer represents a very small minority. In essence, the phone call from the customer is anecdotal, and likely does not represent the population, as no random sample of one ever can.

Because the entrepreneur is often related to or has been long-time friends with some or even most of the employees he has hired, they still may come to him directly with problems and concerns, even if they have a manager or someone else to whom they should report. Entrepreneurs like to fix problems, which can often really be a knee-jerk reaction to one employee's frustration that no one else shares.

For example, imagine the entrepreneur is at a family reunion. A relative that works for his company starts to give him a bad time because the employee thinks the company should fire the sales manager, his boss. The entrepreneur grows more and more frustrated stewing over the issue and is ready to fire the manager when he returns. Upon further investigation, the entrepreneur learns that the relative was actually in the wrong.

In a small company where the entrepreneur knew everything that was happening each day in the business, such a misunderstanding would be impossible. But in small and medium-sized companies that have outgrown their startup entrepreneur's ability to be involved in every detail of the business, it happens all the time. Besides all the wasted time, worry, and resources, the biggest issue this situation causes is a lack of clarity.

Anecdotal information leads to a lack of clarity. It does not represent how the entire company is doing. Here's another example. A successful construction company with over 1,000 employees was the pride of the owner. A few of those employees were skilled mechanics who worked out of a company-owned shop next to the corporate headquarters, servicing the company's fleet of vehicles and equipment. One day the owner of the company pulled into the office and saw the mechanics sitting around with nothing to do. They were enjoying a rare moment when none of the hundreds of vehicles and pieces of equipment had immediate maintenance requirements. He immediately assumed all of the rest of the employees deployed all over the county in which the company operated were doing the same thing, and his business was going to crumble before the day was over.

I know, you're probably thinking there is no way someone with such a large company would make such an assumption. But it happens all the time. A quick look at this company's scoreboards would tell you that it was

166

operating more effectively than it had in years. Sure, improvements could still be made, but this anecdotal information was just that--it was not an accurate snapshot, or representation, of the overall effectiveness of the company.

As we learned in the allegory, the best way for an entrepreneur or business owner to transition to running their business with quantitative data is to implement the six scoreboards every business needs, and those scoreboards need to adhere to the IMAPCT criteria.

27

RELATIONSHIP OF CLARITY TO CASH

Jennifer helps Steve obtain clarity about his business. Clarity in business has to do with three things--the past, the present, and the future. Steve's clarity about his business means he understands, using the IMPACT criteria, where he's been, where he is, and where he's going. Like a three-legged stool depends on all three stools to function properly, removing any one of these elements, the past, present, or future, would damage one's ability to clearly see the whole picture of your business.

FIGURE 27-1

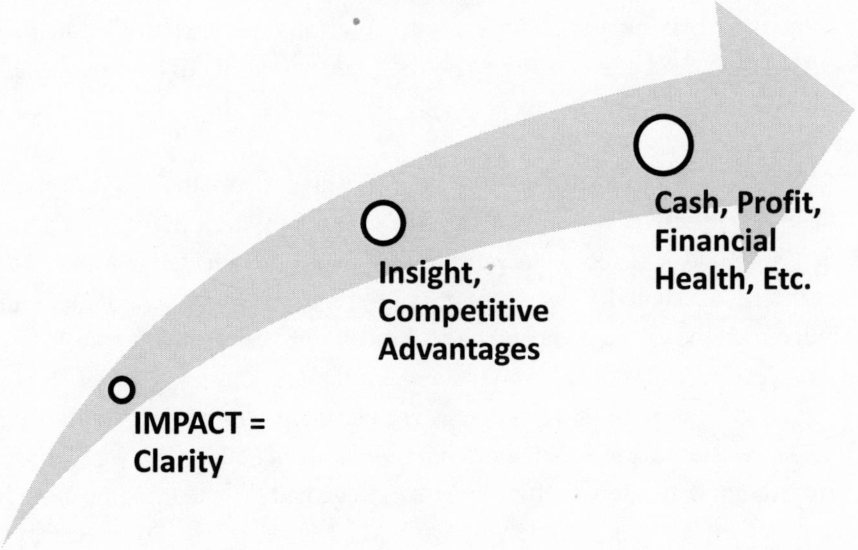

Cash, Profit, Financial Health, Etc.

Insight, Competitive Advantages

IMPACT = Clarity

IMPACT information leads to clarity, which leads to insights, which foster strategic competitive advantages. Those advantages lead to more cash and profit, improved financial health, and a host of other benefits, as demonstrated in Figure 27-1.

When we achieve this clarity, here are the three main benefits we receive, all of which lead to improved cash, profit, financial health, and more:

- Minimize anxiety
- Improve tactical decision-making
- Improve strategic decision-making

BENEFIT 1 – MINIMIZE ANXIETY

Anxiety in a business is usually associated with fear, worry, and uneasiness about potentially undesirable outcomes. For example, a business that is nine months behind with its financial statements may generate some anxiety in those who are running that business. They might know what the balance in their bank account is today, but they have no idea if they are actually profitable and if they can sustain the business in the future.

I was recently introduced to a business experiencing extreme financial difficulties. It did not surprise me to learn that they had not received accurate or timely financial statements in years. They lacked any way to measure their performance historically other than the cash in their bank account, which is almost always a false indicator of how the business is doing. They lacked a way to measure their current productivity and success, and they had no clarity on where they were going and how they intended to get there.

Anxiety in this business was high. It was not until they gained clarity in their past, present, and future that they could create a plan to turn their business around and return to profitability. Not coincidentally, this clarity, even though it painted a very grim picture, reduced everyone's anxiety and reinvigorated the entire company as its key executives created a plan to save the business, working together to make their plan a reality.

Steve began to grasp the negative correlation of anxiety to clarity in Chapter 23. He realized that the anxiety was dispelled by clarity. Jennifer reminded him that when the two first met, Steve had little clarity, meaning he was experiencing great anxiety toward his business. The more clarity a business owner has, the less anxiety he will experience. Concern about the future of the business can never be completely removed. But clarity pushes the worry aside and identifies the problems that really need to be solved. And most business owners and entrepreneurs would much prefer knowing what the problem is so that they can fix it to not even knowing what the problem is in the first place. Figure 27-2 is a simple representation of this inverse relationship.

FIGURE 27-2

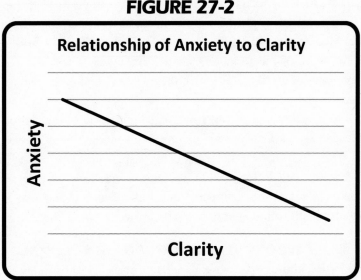

In the allegory, Steve's anxiety at home was also high. As he began to engage more with his family, he began to gain more clarity and, ultimately, direction for how to best accomplish his goals and objectives for his family. The point is that the negative correlation between anxiety and clarity is true in all aspects of life, not just business.

It has been my experience the more clarity an entrepreneur has, the more effectively and successfully they run their business. The relationship between clarity and an entrepreneur's effectiveness, therefore, are positively correlated.

BENEFIT 2 – IMPROVE TACTICAL DECISION-MAKING
You obtain clarity in the past with timely and accurate monthly

financial/managerial reporting along with weekly dashboard reports. You obtain clarity in the present with daily dashboard reports and other productivity and cash management tools. Your clarity in the future comes from a combination of short-term cash flow projections, an annual budget, a 5-year plan, and an up-to-date financial model. Knowing that tactical decisions involve the day-to-day functions in a business, here is an example from one of my customers on how we improved our ability to make tactical decisions with clarity.

In the monthly executive team meeting in which we discuss the past, present, and future of the firm, the President shared that one of the largest customers was requesting a new Request for Proposal (RFP) from all of its vendors for some of the services provided. Included in this request was an entirely new tier of services for which the company had never had to provide unbundled pricing.

Within 30 minutes we constructed an entire financial model to determine the lowest possible prices we could offer without damaging our margins. This information was powerful, especially when the President realized that her competitors would likely have much higher prices than our minimums. The result--her company won the bid with prices that increased our margins but still came in at or below the prices of our competitors.

BENEFIT 3 – IMPROVE STRATEGIC DECISION-MAKING

In addition to improving tactical decision-making and implementation, financial clarity may bring its greatest benefit in terms of driving the strategic direction, or big-picture vision, of a business. Here is just one example:

Another growing company that uses our CFO services became dissatisfied with the performance of its distribution strategy. Sales growth had been less than stellar, to put it nicely. They began to explore different distribution strategies, from wholesale to retail and from manufacturers' reps to an in-house sales team, desiring to be open to all options and suggestions.

Because of the already-existing financial clarity, the process was quite simple--evaluate all of the options and find the distribution strategy that would add the most value to the shareholders. We modeled each option and eventually chose the one with the most promise. Although they are still in the development and implementation phases of this strategic change, they have already received several points of validation, like better-than-expected success in several different test markets, that they are moving in the best direction.

CASH--THE COMMON METRIC

All three of these benefits lead to improved cash flow. Why so much focus on cash? Because it is the single common thread in every business that determines if a company wins or loses. And, ultimately, cash is king.

Every industry, and possibly each business in that industry, will have different indicators and metrics that are its top priority to report and manage. In some way, all of those metrics lead to improving the cash flow of the business. So, ultimately, cash is the final scoreboard. The challenge is that alone it is an unreliable indicator of past, present, and future performance. So we have to use these other scoreboards to help us improve our cash.

The commonality every business shares with cash is validated by the entire process whereby a business can be assessed with a value. In most instances, a business is worth a lot more than its assets minus its debts, liabilities, and other obligations. The way those assets are used to generate cash flow, and the way the liabilities are leveraged to accelerate the cash flow of a business, makes the entire business worth much more than just the net sum of all of its parts.

So how do the experts determine the value of a business? They evaluate the businesses historical ability to generate cash flow along with its prospects for generating cash flow in the future. You may be familiar with a common practice for valuing a business wherein a business determines its EBITDA (Earnings Before Interest, Taxes, Depreciation, and Amortization) and applies a multiple to determine the value of the company. For example, if a business had $1,000,000 in EBITDA in its most recent operating year, and the multiple for that business was four, the business would be worth $4,000,000.

But don't be misled by this EBITDA concept. EBITDA is a shortcut to try and determine the cash flow of a business. That's right--EBITDA is a lazy shortcut to cash flow. The multiple is determined by the prospects of the industry and the individual business to be able to generate future cash.

Another common method used to determine the value of the business is called the Discounted Cash Flow (DCF) model. All this does is estimate the cash flow the company will generate into the future, and then discount it back to present day dollars. The discount rate takes into account the level of confidence the investment community has in this industry and individual business to be able to realize the estimated cash projections. The discount rate usually represents the rate of return the investment community might expect relative to the risk an investor might take by investing in the business.

The common scoreboard of all businesses, even non-profit entities, is cash. Clarity will improve cash, make your business more valuable, and reward you more handsomely for being willing to take the risk of starting the business in the first place.

Even if owning a valuable business is not your primary concern at the moment, this connection between clarity and cash should always be a priority. Clarity will improve your ability to accomplish all of your objectives for your business, because the cash flow it helps you generate will be the fuel to get you where you want to go.

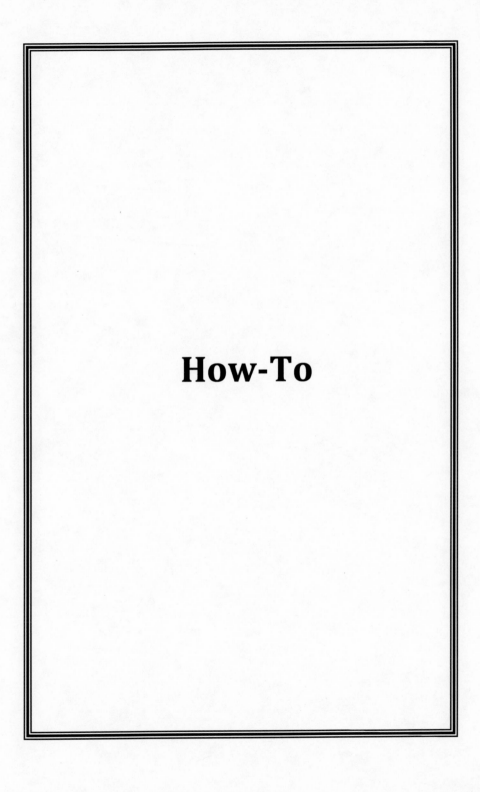

How-To

28
THREE-PIECE PUZZLE

Talking about these reports and projections and all of the benefits businesses receive from them is compelling and meaningful. Implementing everything it takes to get them is an entirely different story, and can be time-consuming and costly. But it doesn't have to be either.

I have found that while each company is different and unique, there are three things that every entrepreneur must balance and bring together in order to create the most effective means for generating IMPACT-level quantitative data. The three pieces of this puzzle are:

- Staff
- Software
- Procedures

PIECE 1: STAFF
I have seen every form of creative and non-creative ways entrepreneurs have tried to staff their accounting and finance functions. Here are the best practices I recommend for any entrepreneur, from start-up to medium-sized enterprise, in order to appropriately staff these disciplines and get the best bang for your buck.

When you first start a company, you will not have a lot of need for historical IMPACT reporting because you are involved in every detail of the business and are gaining the strategic insight you need to improve. However, you still have a compliance need to keep organized records and information, and you may also have a forecasting need, especially if you want to raise debt or equity capital to grow.

So, a startup should hire an outsourced bookkeeper (rates will vary between $25 and $75+ per hour) that spends as little as a few hours per month and as much as a few hours per week to keep a clean set of cash-basis books at a minimum or accrual-based books if at all possible. This is likely what your tax accountant, or CPA, will need (and a clean set of books gets you a less expensive tax return, usually) to prepare your taxes and keep you compliant with federal, state, and local taxing authorities. Either have your bookkeeper, CPA, or payroll processing company handle your payroll and all of its filing and depositing complexities. Sometimes you can get all of this, monthly bookkeeping and payroll, for $100 or less per month, plus the annual cost of a tax return for your business entity.

I am often asked how to best hire an external tax accountant or CPA. In addition to them having the right credentials and experience, the most critical consideration is the care factor. Do they care about you to the extent that they are proactive and try to help you get the most value for the money you spend with them. Some CPAs get too many clients and lose their ability to care, even though they likely have the very best of intentions to do so.

When it comes to forecasting and planning, this will likely be beyond the abilities of your bookkeeper, who is not trained or experienced to think strategically. And if they are, then you're probably overpaying them to be your bookkeeper. Most CPAs are capable, but their practices often do not allow them to be as helpful as you might hope in this process. A finance executive, like Jennifer, who is a CFO-caliber person, is usually the best solution in terms of costs and value-added to your firm. I will discuss this role after I complete the discussion on staffing the accounting and finance department of any sized company.

Any of the functions I have just described can be performed by a spouse, relative, neighbor, or friend, but only if they are qualified. Even if they offer to help you for free, you will likely pay a lot more for the mistakes of inexperience than you ever would for doing it right the first time. One of my favorite quotes to validate this point comes from an anonymous source: "If you think it's expensive to hire a professional, wait until you see how expensive it is to clean up after you hire an amateur."

As the startup grows, the company should begin to look to hire part or full-time clerical staff to handle most of the AR, AP, and payroll tasks, usually positions at $15/hour or less, while the bookkeeper remains part-time and delegates everything they possibly can to the in-house staff. You'll know you've reached this point if your part-time bookkeeper can't keep up or your accounting costs start to get too high, more than twenty hours per week times their billable rate. This follows a simple division of labor procedure, filling up the lowest cost employees with as much as they can intellectually handle and then having higher cost employees, the ones with more education, background, experience, and training in accounting and finance, do the higher-level tasks.

At this level the company may still only need cash-basis accounting, and that is directly correlated to the entrepreneur's ability to keep up with all of the details of the day-to-day operations. Once he doesn't personally know all of the customers, employees, and/or vendors and suppliers, it's probably time to look at accrual accounting (which reports on actual performance, without regard for when cash actually flows in and out of the bank), which will mean you will potentially need a little more firepower in your accounting department. But I'll get into that more in a minute.

So, as the company continues to grow, things become more complex--more products, more services, more employees, more locations, etc. You will continue to maximize the work your lowest cost employees perform, but now they need more leadership and direction as well as systems and processes to follow to allow you to adhere to the IMPACT criteria of getting data to run your business.

Perhaps your bookkeeper can handle this, but often they even need help. This, again, is where the services of someone like Jennifer, an outsourced CFO, can add value at very little cost. As you fill out your accounting and finance department, your bookkeeper will eventually not be able to keep up with the workload. This is when you need to let your bookkeeper go and hire an accounting manager or controller. This person should have a degree in accounting and know debits and credits (accounting terminology) extremely well.

This full-time hire will be a significant step in the progression of your firm as you are developing an in-house competency to generate IMPACT information. But you will likely still need the help of a senior-level executive on an outsourced basis. You should never hire a full-time CFO before a controller. The reason is basic. With no controller, the CFO will have to do lower-level work and you will not be getting as much value for having a member of your strategic executive team mired down in the detail of all of the numbers all day long.

As your firm grows beyond this point, you will hire more staff at various levels until you need a full-time CFO. You will let your outsourced finance executive go, or maybe keep them on your board of directors or in some other advisory capacity, and fill that position with a full-time person.

My experience has taught me that a lot of entrepreneurs don't even know what CFO stands for, let alone the benefits one can bring to their organizations. So, I have included excerpts of an article I recently wrote which lists the ten attributes your finance executive should possess if you are considering adding this position, either in a part or full-time capacity.

What makes a great Chief Financial Officer? How can a CEO know if they are getting everything they should from their part-time CFO? These ten attributes are a big part of what you would find common with every CFO who adds great value to their company, staff, and community. For the sake of simplicity, I will assume the CFO is male. Please do not mistake my choice of gender with one's ability to be a great CFO. I know many women, like Jennifer from the allegory, that fill this role effectively and successfully!

1. A decade or more of senior-level experience: He needs to have been around the block a little bit as an executive, and other C-level roles are helpful (like Chief Executive Officer, Chief Operations Officer, etc). He has done significant debt and equity financing transactions as well as guided successful entries and exits for shareholders.

2. Both breadth and depth of knowledge and experience: While industry knowledge is valuable, a big part of his ability to add value to your firm will be his experiences in and around a multiple of industries. He will possess the unique ability to understand and lead several, if not all, of the disciplines (including operations, human resources, IT, and even sales and marketing) of the company with great focus and precision. He needs to have significant experience helping companies obtain clarity, maximize cash, improve profits, and optimize their resources from a multi-disciplinary perspective.

3. Honest, ethical, and personification of integrity: These values cannot be understated. The CFO works in a world that few outside of it understand. If he abuses that in any way, then he jeopardizes too much. He needs to be a person you look to who will always 'shoot-straight.'

4. People person, not just a number-cruncher: His people need to like and trust him, and he needs to inspire them to improve and grow while they build and add value to the company. He also needs to be someone who you are confident can represent your company with investors, bankers, and other professionals. Some accountants and professionals do not enjoy working with a lot of people and collaborating for success. These types will never be successful CFOs.

5. Strategist and Visionary: He is always thinking ahead. Reporting on the past is an important function he oversees, but his greatest value will come from his foresight and ability to strategically guide the company as a whole, not as individual parts.

6. Relationships with the investment and banking communities: He should know them, and they should know him. His reputation should precede him. He should be able to open new doors of opportunity and new schools of thought to his company in this area.

7. Open to new opportunities; flexible: If he always says no before hearing you out, then he will never succeed as the CFO. In the broad and deep context of all of his experience and strategy for the company, he should be able to filter through opportunities and help the company implement the ones that best position the company to achieve its objectives and improve its competitive advantages in the market.

8. Continual quest to learn and stay ahead: The worlds of finance, accounting, tax, and business are dynamic and always changing. Ask him what the last business book he read was and what he gained from it. If it was his accounting class textbook from twenty years ago, then he's probably not on the cutting-edge of where the company and his stewardship need to go.

9. Diplomatic and persuasive: The CFO holds all of the confidential and valuable components to the business model and plans for growth. In some ways he is the protector of them. He needs to carefully and professionally work with others around him without being abrasive but uses persuasive communication to engender buy-in and loyalty. These are sometimes rare traits, but a great CFO needs them desperately.

10. CEO's most trusted advisor; powerful resource to the board: Before the CEO moves on any critical decision, he should be in the CFOs office to discuss it. The CFO should offer advice and direction to help the CEO make sound and effective decisions in the leadership of the firm. If the CEO and the board of directors avoid the CFO, then he will not last very long.

PIECE 2: SOFTWARE
Software does not solve problems. People and systems solve problems, then software simplifies and automates those solutions for greater efficiency and performance. Software is an important piece of the puzzle, but not the whole puzzle.

You should not initially buy a business metric, dashboard, accounting, or ERP (Enterprise Resource Planning) software program thinking it will manage itself. You need to start by assessing what your needs are and what people and processes you will have to design, implement, and support your software purchase. This will ensure you maximize your purchase.

Go through your entire organization and create a wish list and a must-have list based on the needs and wants of your entire organization. Then start searching for the best fit. Most small companies will find QuickBooks or other 'off-the-shelf' programs are more than sufficient for their needs. But even these programs that are marketed as 'easy-to-use' need the right staff and processes to generate reports that adhere to the IMPACT criteria.

Emerging and medium-sized companies usually upgrade to a more robust version of QuickBooks or move to a more comprehensive ERP system. These programs require even more qualified staff to run them and usually even more comprehensive policies and procedures.

PIECE 3: PROCEDURES
I know, just the word 'procedures' makes entrepreneurs cringe. You want to be out growing your business and developing new products and services to take better care of your current customers and attract new ones. Procedures take time to create, they require a lot of attention to detail, and your business is changing so fast that you may outgrow your most up-to-date procedures within the next six months.

So why bother to create procedures for the accounting and finance functions of your business? There are really three reasons: consistency, efficiency, and checks and balances.

Nothing is more frustrating than having to recreate the wheel every time you go through an accounting transaction, especially one that's complex. It requires a great deal of mental bandwidth, and chances are you'll do it a little differently than the time you had to handle a similar transaction a few months earlier. By creating procedures for all of your transactions, your accounting will become consistent, which falls under the Precise definition of the IMPACT criteria.

In addition to consistency, procedures will help with efficiency. By creating a standardized way to handle each transaction in your business, you can hire less expensive staff to handle them, including all or almost all of the day-to-day functions. And, it means you're developing a competency all your own, which will help you more successfully execute your business model and accelerate your reporting capabilities.

The last reason to establish accounting and finance procedures has to do with implementing appropriate checks and balances to minimize your exposure to embezzlement, fraud, and theft. I believe most people are honest. Yet with the right amount of opportunity, even the best are tempted to steal from their employer. This is why every business, regardless of its size, needs to have some internal controls and procedures in place to protect the company and its honest employees.

The examples of employee theft and embezzlement are far too many to cite. But most of us have heard at least one horror story. I met the owner of a company last year who had an employee, a trusted family member, embezzle over $1,000,000 from the company. And this employee was an upright member of the community known for being honest. So how did this happen?

It starts with a company that gives more and more control in the accounting and finance functions to just one person. Phrases like: "I would trust him with my life," and "I know I can trust him – he is honest and loyal to me," become the basis for giving too much control. The challenge is that the more control someone has, the greater the temptation becomes to steal because no one is looking and no one will notice.

As the temptation grows for the employee, he or she begins to have more of an entitlement mentality toward the employer. They may have thoughts like: "I deserve to take this from the company because I've been working overtime for six months with no extra pay or bonus." I was once part of terminating an employee who had stolen fuel from a company. His response was that he had worked some overtime and, instead of putting it on his time sheet he thought he would just make up for it by taking a little fuel. Again, entitlement begins to creep in.

Once the employee gets away with a little theft, it can become addicting. They become so entrenched in the lies they are living they begin to distance themselves from reality with overwhelming justifications for their behavior.

So, how can you avoid problem? First, please know that there are many people who are dishonest and will try to steal from you no matter what controls you put in place. With that as a disclaimer, you should consider some of these suggestions as low-cost alternatives to trusting just one person with all of the controls:

- Consider separating the activities of creating invoices, receiving payments, applying payments, opening bank statements, and reconciling bank statements between at least two people. Even if you need to have someone work a couple of hours a month on a couple of these functions, it could be well worth it.
- Regularly audit your customer and vendor list to validate they are real.
- Regularly audit payroll by verifying the existence of and value added by all employees.
- If you or your employees handle cash, put systems in place to hold those employees accountable for every penny they touch.

These are just a few suggestions, and there are many more. By establishing the right procedures and controls in your business in a cost-effective manner, you will be taking steps that will help protect you, your company, and your employees.

In order to help you see how these three pieces come together to complete the puzzle, I have prepared three examples--one of a startup, another of a small but growing company, and a third of an emerging or medium-sized company.

EXAMPLE 1: A STARTUP

You should not be focused on becoming an expert in accounting, nor should you be spending your time trying to enter and code accounting transactions or reconciling bank accounts. The most effective use of your time will be trying to land your first customers and establish proof of concept for your company. As far as staff, you should find an outsourced bookkeeper who can handle all of the necessary accounting and finance functions for you, and consider an outsourced CFO if you are raising capital or need to model your future performance for some other reason.

You can rely on a simple, off-the-shelf accounting program like QuickBooks for all of your basic needs, although you may want to supplement your business functions with other SaaS programs for invoicing, project and time management, and more. Have your bookkeeper establish your basic accounting procedures as part of his or her duties.

EXAMPLE 2: SMALL BUT GROWING COMPANY

It will no longer make sense to have your bookkeeper entering all of your transactions. It is too expensive and you can hire someone in-house for less cost. That new hire can begin to build your accounting and finance competencies. At this stage a part-time CFO can begin to add real value to the strategic direction of your firm as well as the processes for implementing the six IMPACT scoreboards.

A simple off-the-shelf software program will still do the trick, although you will find you are beginning to push its limits. By putting more procedures in place, you will maintain your consistency even though more hands are involved in entering and reconciling your books.

EXAMPLE 3: EMERGING COMPANY

You will likely need to replace your bookkeeper with a full-time Accounting Manager or Controller, and you will be adding additional clerks and other role players to the accounting and administrative functions. Your dependence on a part-time CFO will become even more critical as you face complexities and issues that require a seasoned finance executive to manage and solve.

At this stage you will likely outgrow most off-the-shelf software programs and need to move to a more robust ERP system. Your Controller will become the in-house expert on the system, and the development of your firm's procedures to support the new system, the ongoing reporting requirements, and the increased complexities will help your competencies in accounting and finance blossom.

CONCLUSION: THE COMPLETE PUZZLE

The point of discussing this three-piece puzzle is to help entrepreneurs know how to best structure their organizations to get the information they need. I do not recommend that an entrepreneur focus solely on these initiatives. In fact, the entrepreneur's efforts are usually best spent in other areas of the company, like new product development or business development.

The entrepreneur's role is to get help determining exactly what he needs, then put the right people in place to source, implement, and execute the appropriate staff, software, and procedure plans to minimize the costs but maximize the output of the accounting and finance function of the company.

29

IMPACT THE PAST AND PRESENT

The Monthly, Weekly, and Daily IMPACT Indicators™ are three main scoreboards that help business owners and entrepreneurs gain the clarity they need regarding their past and present. In this chapter I will discuss all three, including the most common mistakes I see when companies try to implement these principles.

Monthly IMPACT Indicators™
Of all of the six scoreboards, this is usually the one that I start within a company. The reason is simple; from it stems most of what you need to accomplish the other five, if you are doing the other five correctly. Table 29-1 summarizes how to make sure the Monthly IMPACT Indicators™ meet the IMPACT criteria. There are three steps in this process: close the month, prepare and analyze the reporting package, then meet to discuss the results, findings, observations, and recommendations.

First, you need to close your books after each month is completed and reconciled. This includes a comprehensive reconciliation of each balance sheet account, including things like inventory, cash, payroll liabilities, loan balances, and more. Most companies are not doing this, so here is some more detail on how to go about it.

Create a procedure for reconciling each balance sheet account. Reconciling means to validate the balance you have in your accounting software with some other independent source. For example, reconciling your bank account refers to ensuring the balance you show in your books matches the balance on the statement you receive from the bank, transaction-by-transaction. A similar procedure needs to exist for each account, and the backup detail of each reconciliation process should be saved or stored in a safe place each month.

TABLE 29-1

Monthly IMPACT Indicators™		
I	Insightful	Increase financial knowledge; organize information based on business model; review and discuss with executive team; generate strategic insight
M	Meaningful	Focus on pivotal performance drivers--job-costing, product mix, gross margin, overhead, current ratio, DSO, and more; package of ten or more pages
P	Precise	Reconcile all balance sheet accounts; reconcile all profit & loss accounts; use accrual accounting
A	Accessible	Physical--email, print, put on wall, confidential; Intellectual--charts and graphs, spend time discussing and analyzing
C	Comparative	Compare to last month, year-to-date, same month last several years, year-to-date last several years, Annual and 5-Year IMPACT Forecaster™
T	Timely	Available by the 15th or 20th of the following month

After you reconcile all of the balance sheet accounts, you need to review all of the transactions on the profit and loss statements. The best way to do this is to run a report that allows you to look at the activity in each account for at least the last six months. Make sure rent is not doubled up in any months, and determine the root causes for any other anomalies or trends that seem out of line with the normal operations of the business.

I have analyzed or looked at the financial statements of hundreds of companies, and they are almost never accurate. Here are some areas that I most commonly find issues:

- Cash basis reporting
- Incorrect revenue recognition
- Gross margin varies by more than 3% month-to-month
- Reporting is not broken-down by division, job, or product
- Other costs are not recognized correctly
- Accounts receivable have old, uncollectable accounts
- Inventory is wrong, with lack of a physical count being one of the main reasons for such
- Fixed Assets are not booked correctly
- Depreciation is either not booked or only booked on an accelerated tax basis
- Payroll liabilities are wrong
- Debt payments are incorrectly coded
- The equity section is off
- Owner compensation is not handled correctly

Are any of these a problem for you? Don't let them keep you from creating IMPACT information that will bring you the clarity you need to help your business.

You should finish the balance sheet and profit and loss statement reconciliations by the 10th, or maybe the 12th of the next month. Once you are sure everything is entered into your accounting system, it's accurate, and it's reconciled, you need to close your books. This means you lock up that month and all prior months so that no information or data may be altered in any way. Almost every accounting system has the ability to do this. If you're not currently using this function, then begin using it immediately.

Now that everything is accurate and locked, it's time to create the reports that should be in the Monthly IMPACT Indicators™ package. While every business' needs will be a little different, here are some of the reports that every package should include each month:

- Comparative balance sheet
- Balance sheet ratio analysis and charting, including liquidity, Days Sales Outstanding (DSO), and more.
- Profit and Loss statement (P&L) for the current month and YTD with percentages of sales
- Comparative P&L with prior months, prior years, and industry
- Charts and graphs to show trends in relevant areas of the P&L
- Managerial reporting on profit drivers in the business
- Budget vs. Actual variance analysis, sometimes for up to three different budget scenarios
- Statement of cash flow
- Charts and Graphs to show trends in relevant areas of cash flow

Now that the reports are created and put into a package, you need analysis done from the perspective of a financial executive who knows your business. This analysis is often communicated in several ways, including a cover sheet as well as comments, notes, arrows, and highlights throughout the package.

With the reports and analysis in all of the key players' hands, you need to have a meeting to discuss the month. When the reporting package meets the IMPACT criteria, I have yet to see where this meeting does not foster a strategic discussion that ends up benefiting the firm in some way. There are lots of business experts who tell you to have fewer meetings. Do not cut this one out. It should be the most beneficial meeting you have all month.

Weekly IMPACT Indicators™

In Chapter 21, Jennifer shared the analogy with Steve of being stranded on a deserted island with only one piece of paper each week to run his business. When you remove the subjective elements of running a business and try to do it on objective data alone, how does that change your ability to make the right decisions?

Initially, trying to rely on quantitative data to run your business is a hard thing to do, even if you're still absorbing qualitative information, too. That's why designing the weekly metrics you need to run your business needs a perspective you may not be able to attain alone. You have to think outside of the way you currently do things.

Weekly IMPACT Indicators™ (please see Table 29-2 for the IMPACT criteria for this report) are often referred to as a flash, dashboard, or KPI reports. KPI stands for Key Performance Indicators. Regardless of what you call it, it should be critical in assisting you predict sales, cash flow and profit and gain clarity on the performance and direction of the company. In addition, it should be an essential decision-making tool used in the day-to-day operation of the firm that empowers you to make the best decisions for your company that will drive cash flow and profitability.

There are three main steps to consider in building an effective Weekly IMPACT Indicators™ report.

- First, you should know the averages and benchmarks for your business as well as others in the same industry.
- Second, you need to determine the best one to three metrics per department/discipline within your company to measure.
- Third, you should go back and pull as much data as you can for all of those metrics historically to see what you learn and gain from the numbers. This will help you initially determine the metrics you should include on the report. And if you have a hard time limiting your metrics to three, go ahead and include more to start. Then you can cut back once you see which are the most helpful.

Before I cover the different departments/disciplines in the business and how to start figuring out which metrics will be the best, I need to briefly discuss a trend I am seeing with software, both downloaded and online SaaS applications. There seems to be a lot of people and experts talking about buying software to track your metrics, or maybe your accounting software is adding and upgrading features to give you a dashboard for your business.

While I love the way these programs improve accessibility, they come inherent with many challenges. Without the proper procedures and staff in place, this software often struggles to be precise or meaningful. Just pulling information from your accounting system does not guarantee its accuracy, and I've seen many businesses be misled because they weren't looking at accurate information.

Also, these systems generally come with some common metrics and reports, but those pre-canned numbers are often not the most helpful or meaningful to the business. So, software is good, but it needs the help of the right staff and processes to make sure it is designed and then implemented with attention to all of the IMPACT criteria.

To keep this simple, I will break the different departments and disciplines of your business into four main categories, with many businesses needing to track sub-categories and completely different categories also. Marketing, sales, operations, and financial are the four main categories every business needs to include if you want the dashboard to adequately inform you on your deserted island.

MAREKTING: Marketing is about lead generation--all of the activities in which you engage to get your message and value proposition, your brand, to the market. And this is where your weekly reports should begin. After all, it's where your customers start in their life-cycle with you as well. You need leads if you ever hope of acquiring customers.

Your Weekly IMPACT Indicators™ should include the top two or three metrics for measuring your lead generation. These may include number of visits to your website and percentage of those visitors that become qualified leads. The key here is to focus on the processes you are currently employing to market and generate leads and measure the efficacy of those efforts. The cost of acquiring a lead should be included if it is measurable, and it almost always is.

SALES: Obviously a lead is still useless if you cannot convert it into a paying customer. Conversion of leads to customers is a critical element of your weekly report. In addition, total sales should be included so you know how your volume is doing on at least a weekly basis. Sales should be communicated in terms of dollars, number of sellable units, and average pricing.

OPERATIONS: Your sales department is responsible to turn the leads into paying customers, and operations desires to satisfy and retain the customers as long as possible. Most business models try to accomplish this by structuring and delivering everything you promise for as little cost as possible. As such, operational effectiveness is what you usually want to measure on your weekly report. Since this differs by industry and business, here are a few examples.

If you are a professional service firm that is mainly selling time in exchange for services, then you are likely concerned about your average cost of paying staff per hour as it relates to your average revenue per hour. You will also be very concerned with ratios like revenue per employee and sales-to-wages.

If you manufacture products, then you will want to understand the efficiency of all of your inputs, including materials (and scrap), labor, contractors, and other direct costs. In essence, you need to look at the major determinants of your gross margin.

You will want to consider three additional metrics on your weekly report that deal with operations. First, an indicator of your current utilization of your total available capacity, remembering that operating at maximum capacity creates the best profit scenario for your business. Second, customer satisfaction and retention metrics are valuable barometers for ongoing sales. And, third, a measure of product or service quality levels.

FINANCIAL: The marketing, sales, and operations lead to your financial performance. And you will benefit by seeing some of your financial metrics on your weekly report. You need to know what is happening with all of your major current assets, which usually includes cash, accounts receivable (AR), and inventory. You should quantify the performance of AR in terms of total % over 60 days past due as well as the Days Sales Outstanding (DSO). You should also understand if your inventory levels are at efficient levels.

You will also likely want to include some of your current liabilities, like accounts payable and line of credit balances. This information leads to the tracking of the firm's current ratio on a weekly basis and other versions of the current ratio that traditionally predict cash flow with some accuracy.

If you received a weekly dashboard report with all of the information above (tailored to your industry and business model), how well do you think you could manage your business from a deserted island? Now, you should imagine having all of that information every week along with being in your business every day, collecting qualitative information as well. Not only will your anxiety decrease and your strategic insights increase, you will feel empowered to make the right decisions to improve cash, profits, and financial health. Even if the weekly report has bad news, knowing about it will still reduce your anxiety because you will at least have the opportunity to do something about it before it becomes worse.

TABLE 29-2

Weekly IMPACT Indicators™		
I	Insightful	One-page of everything you need to run your business remotely; gain insights in marketing, sales, operations, finance, and more
M	Meaningful	Include 1-3 of most meaningful metrics from each discipline; focus on key performance drivers for each department/division
P	Precise	Use right mix of staff, software, and procedures to produce; ensure integrity of sources and accuracy of information precise
A	Accessible	Physical--body of email, software login, posted on wall; Intellectual--charts and graphs focused on trends, highs, and lows
C	Comparative	4-week, 13-week, 26-week, and 52-week rolling averages; comparisons to last several periods and Quarterly IMPACT Forecaster™
T	Timely	Available by Monday of the following week.

Here is a simple ten step process for establishing your Weekly IMPACT Indicators™. Please do not feel overwhelmed by this list. Remember that using the three-piece puzzle of staff, software, and procedures will make this possible. As an example, I had this entire report up and running in less than two weeks for a manufacturing company, and the executives of the company love it. It is part of their weekly management meetings.

First, don't buy a dashboard or other software tool. This step needs to wait – remember, software does not solve problems. People, processes, and intelligence solve problems, then software automates and simplifies the solution.

Second, make a list of what you think will be important to track each week. There should be key metrics from marketing, sales, operations, and finance, other departments and business disciplines in your organization on your list.

Third, create an Excel spreadsheet, or a Google doc spreadsheet for those of you living in the cloud, and list each of the things you want to track across the top to create several columns. Then, list the Friday of each of the following 52 weeks down the left-hand column titled "Week Ending."

Fourth, coordinate with your team where all of the information will come from for this document. It may need to come from several people, so commit them to get the information to you on time and in the format that will work best for you.

Fifth, start tracking all of these metrics for four weeks and see what everyone thinks. What information do they like? What information is missing, and what could be added to reduce anxiety and fear? Then repeat this process for the next three months.

Sixth, once you feel you have your list of items you want on your dashboard pretty well-defined, start to investigate the best ways to automate the collection of this information into your weekly dashboard. The information will likely come from many different software applications, including your accounting system, your CRM, and more.

Seven, start to investigate dashboard SaaS tools based on their ability to pull data from all of your sources. You may find this needs to include some manual input, or it may make the most sense to do it all manually in the spreadsheet you started with.

Eight, purchase a dashboard that solves the highest number of issues in terms of automation, timeliness, and accuracy. Or, if you like the spreadsheet you are using, create some charts and graphs that update each time you update the document with a new week's data.

Nine, start tracking 4-week, 13-week, 26-week, and 52-week rolling averages to help you spot key trends in the data.

Ten, sit back and enjoy the fruits of your labors with the critical information you need to run your business right at your fingertips. You will be amazed as your anxiety decreases and your strategic insights increase.

Daily IMPACT Indicators™

'Did you win or lose today?' was the question Jennifer asked Steve. So I ask the question, in slightly different form, to you. How do you know if you win or lose each day in your business? When you're leaving for home at the end of your day or else arriving at your office first thing the next morning, how do you know if you accomplished what you should have?

There are a lot of opinions on whether or not daily metrics are valuable enough to expend the effort and resources to track them each day. And, there are also a lot of opinions on what metrics should be measured daily. Based on my experience with lots of different small and medium-sized business in every industry imaginable, I want to tell you what I've found to be the best practices for companies like yours.

First, daily reporting becomes more valuable the bigger and more complex your organization grows. As qualitative information becomes more anecdotal and less reliable in terms of indicating anything close to what is really going on within your company, your need for and dependence upon daily reporting will grow. They are positively correlated. The bigger you get, the more you need IMPACT daily reports.

Detailed and exhaustive daily reports are almost never helpful for small and medium-sized business. The information captured on the Weekly and Monthly IMPACT Indicators™ usually is all you will need in terms of covering all aspects of your business. But what is helpful to see on a daily basis is a report with one to three of your most critical metrics.

In the allegory, Jennifer helped Steve define what his three most important daily metrics were--gross profit, overhead, and changes to backlog, or the balance of the future work of the company. This information truly empowered Steve to know if he won or lost every day. He knew if his projects were covering his operating expenses and, if they were, by how much. He also could glean an impression of how his future was shaping up.

TABLE 29-3

Daily IMPACT Indicators™		
I	Insightful	Did you win or lose today? Gain insights real-time and make strategic and tactical decisions timely
M	Meaningful	Include 1-3 metrics for entire company; focus on core business model performance
P	Precise	Need to make estimates; cannot rely on data straight from software
A	Accessible	Physical--body of email, software login, posted on wall; Intellectual--charts and graphs focused on trends, highs, and lows
C	Comparative	Compare to prior day, week, month, and year for several periods; scrutinize against projection assumptions
T	Timely	Available by morning of the next day

Just from these three numbers, Steve would gain insight into what he could improve and where the company could do better. His weekly report would give him more detail in a timely enough manner that he could catch and correct any negative trends or other problems before they got out of control or could hurt the company in a material way.

So, how can you establish daily reporting that will add value to your business? You need to start with determining what your one to three numbers are. Retail stores often measure gross profit per customer visit and total number of customer visits. Manufacturing facilities may benefit from similar measurements of gross profit totals. Table 29-3 summarizes how to make this daily report meet the IMPACT standard.

But you can see a trend, I hope. You need to be concerned with bringing in enough volume and the right gross margin to hit your objectives for your business. Steve was just happy to see that he was generating enough gross profit to break even, but hopefully your goals are a lot better than that.

In addition, you will benefit from having some way to see how much sales volume you can expect in the future. This is very difficult to measure in retail, although those that have layaway and similar programs are securing sales revenue for the future. Manufacturing and even service businesses, especially those that have to bid for work and work under certain contractual agreements for their customers, can use a number similar to backlog to see where they are headed.

I have been the part-time CFO of a construction business for almost five years. Recently their backlog dropped to the lowest level in a long time. They had less than two months of work, and then the company would have shut down. But the managers and owner of that business did an amazing job contracting new projects, and their backlog went up almost ten times just a few months later. Without the actionable data that from a Daily IMPACT Indicator™, this company may have realized their problem too late.

30

IMPACT THE FUTURE

How many forecasts do you keep concurrently in your company? If the answer is zero, then you have some serious work to do. But if your answer is one, you may be falling well short of what is necessary in difficult economic times, or in any economic climate, for that matter.

Here is a real story of a conversation I had with a banker in the last six months about a customer of our CFO firm. My customer needed to finance some heavy growth and the customer wanted to try to use only bank financing to accomplish this growth. The banker was concerned, primarily because the financing request was going to push the bank to the very limits they would ever, under any circumstances, loan to one company.

He said: "Ken, I have your projections in front of me, and I understand they are conservative, but I'm not going to feel comfortable about this deal until you can show me convincingly that a 25% downturn in this company's top-line will not kill this company and leave the bank high and dry." I agreed to re-work our forecasts based on his request, and I went ahead and ran an additional model with 25% additional growth on top of the already projected growth trends. In about two hours we went from one forecast to three, and the exercise was overwhelmingly valuable.

Creating three plans, one, a realistic version along with, two, a worst-case, and three, a best-case scenario, has become a requirement to run a business, whether your finances are suspect or not. And the stakes are high – if you skimp on the ever-important planning for each scenario, you can quickly get out of control and cause harm, possibly irreparable in nature, to the business.

Financial modeling, forecasting, and budgeting is an exercise that ultimately only proves beneficial if you use the information to validate or invalidate your assumptions, make necessary and timely changes in your business, and continue to try and stay ahead strategically of where you, your competitors, and your industry are going. I will briefly discuss the three of the six scoreboards that every business needs to gain clarity for the future.

Quarterly IMPACT Forecaster™

Most businesses fail to plan for and manage the short-term peaks and valleys of cash flow every business experiences. Using a simple spreadsheet is often the best way to begin to tackle this critical task.

This needs to look at least 90 days into the future, and it needs to break the cash inflows and outflows down on a weekly basis. Don't forget to compare the actual cash flow results from each week to your projections to improve your assumptions each week. Table 30-1 explains the IMPACT standard for this scoreboard.

Organize your cash inflows by customer, if possible. Determine how long it takes to collect from each customer, on average, if your customer list isn't too long. If you have hundreds or thousands of customers, separate them into payment classes such as credit card sales, cash, net 15, net 30, and so on. Schedule when you are expecting to receive payment for your existing receivables, and then project the collections of your sales projections based on their relative payment class or the average collection performance for each customer.

Split your cash outflows into two categories: fixed and variable. Tie the variable outflows to your projections and your fixed outflows to you contracts and past payments, including debt payments and regular distributions to owners, if there are any. Don't forget taxes and other quarterly, annual, and irregular cash outflows.

A good place to verify you have accounted for all of your cash outflows is the bank account. Scour through each transaction in each bank account for the last few months to ensure you included each outflow in your forecast. This exercise will help you determine which expenses are fixed and which are variable, and it will also help you pinpoint the driver for each, improving your assumptions, and, therefore, the accuracy of your forecast.

The website will have samples and templates you can view and download to help you implement this critical dashboard for your business.

TABLE 30-1

Quarterly IMPACT Forecaster™		
I	Insightful	Highlight cash flow shortages and excesses for at least the next 90 days; drive insights to improve working capital cycle
M	Meaningful	Illuminate weekly cash flow drivers, like customer collection, fixed outflows, variable outflows, and financing transactions
P	Precise	Make assumptions based on validated historical performance
A	Accessible	Physical--spreadsheet, software login; Intellectual--hide minutia, emphasize charts and graphs of key drivers
C	Comparative	Compare to prior periods; analyze variance from projection and improve assumptions, if necessary
T	Timely	Organized weekly and available by Monday of following week

Annual IMPACT Forecaster™

I've heard this statement more often than I care to admit: "I cannot predict the future so a budget would be worthless for my business."

I have and will continue to make this guarantee to any business in

201

any industry anywhere in the world: if you follow the "best practices" steps to creating a financial plan and an operating budget for the next twelve months, or Annual IMPACT Forecaster™, and you track your monthly progress every month for twelve months against that plan, you will know more about your business than 80% of your competitors know about theirs.

Why can I make that promise? Because the things learned in that twelve months are so revealing in terms of the most effective business model for what you're trying to accomplish that you cannot help but begin to develop and implement the right strategies for making the business more successful, not to mention other competitive advantages that are commonly gained throughout this process.

Why do most businesses neglect this process? The two main reasons are, first, lack of discipline and, second, lack of resources. This process requires disciplined time, including reviewing your results against your budget EVERY month. It's important to take this one step at a time. It may seem overwhelming at first, but once you have your system in place and do it a few times, it will become a habit to which you may become addicted.

The focus of this monthly analysis should be on the variances. The budget is worthless if you don't do this. You need to know why you varied from your budget. What can you learn from that? Which assumption did you make that did not come to pass? What can you change to improve your performance in that area?

Some companies lack the resources to be able to analyze their historical data and then easily track their progress. Perhaps they do not have an accounting system in place, or perhaps they do not have anyone that knows how to properly operate their system. The accuracy of the numbers is certainly a critical element to making the budgeting process a successful experience. So, having the right staff, a functioning accounting system, and procedures for creating and tracking the Annual IMPACT Forecaster™ are critical to this process. Even QuickBooks allows its users to enter in budget information and run reports to track monthly progress and variances.

If anyone reading this doubts me, I challenge you to take the Annual IMPACT Forecaster™ challenge for twelve months. In my experience as a part-time CFO for many emerging companies, the value derived from the budgeting and reporting process has repeatedly and dramatically improved the bottom-line of every company that implements these principles and best practices. I'm confident you'll experience similar results. It will make your disciplined time worth every penny spent, and then some.

An Annual IMPACT Forecaster™, with IMPACT criteria in Table 30-2, needs to include more than just a P&L. You should project your balance sheet performance as well. And, with each account from your balance sheet budgeted for the next twelve months, you can also project, with surprising accuracy, your statement of cash flows as well.

TABLE 30-2

Annual IMPACT Forecaster™		
I	Insightful	Includes P&L, Balance Sheet, Statement of Cash Flow, and supporting detail; insights come in understanding key assumptions and in variance analysis
M	Meaningful	Month-by-month performance by general ledger account; focus on critical performance drivers for each account
P	Precise	Assumptions founded in historical as well as benchmarked data; all three financial statements tie and balance
A	Accessible	Physical--spreadsheet or software program; Intellectual--summarized information in charts and graphs
C	Comparative	Compare to prior periods; analyze variance from projection and improve assumptions, if necessary
T	Timely	Reviewed and updated monthly

Yes, your budget should include all three of the main financial statements. Each of these three reports appeals more to different groups, but effective businesses use all three to their advantage. The Profit & Loss is usually the focus of entrepreneurs, who disregard the balance sheet and statement of cash flows because they are confusing for those without a lot of education and training in accounting practices. Bankers are usually infatuated with the balance sheet because it is the measure of a company's overall financial health. The statement of cash flows is a favorite among investors, because the intrinsic value of your business is revealed in its ability to generate cash from certain activities, which are illuminated on this report.

With the next twelve months planned from a cash flow, profitability, and financial health perspective, you will be ready to take on the year as well as make adjustments and changes promptly when assumptions in your projections change.

As an example of how your company can benefit from your annual projection, consider what this entrepreneur experienced. A successful software company I work with lost a very significant customer. The initial projections for the impact this would have on the business were devastating. There was no way the business would be able to survive. The entrepreneur made a few reductions to soften the financial blow, and then started spending all of his time selling, trying desperately to bring on new customers to replace the one leaving.

This entrepreneur made an amazing discovery during this process, one that he should have realized a lot early. When he devoted his time to sales, the company brought on a lot of new customers. Within just a few months he single-handedly had almost completely replenished the lost revenue from the one customer who left with revenues from dozens of new customers, a significant upgrade in their customer concentration percentages. They became less dependent on any one customer, reducing their risk and improving the overall value of their business.

Just like this entrepreneur experienced, having an annual forecast and then tracking your progress against it will help you quickly adjust your business to turn whatever challenges or opportunities that present themselves to your benefit. And it will also help you find new strategic opportunities as a result.

As mentioned in the introduction of this section, it is very appropriate to create three or even more forecasts for the year. As the year progresses, you can gravitate toward one or two based on which ones you are the closest to achieving. This will help you to know where your staffing levels and other costs should be, how much you can have in your marketing budget, and much more.

5-Year IMPACT Forecaster™
The 5-Year forecast is a month-by-month and summarized year-by-year projection of the P&L, balance sheet, and statement of cash flows. It should be your best representation of what will happen in the future, hopefully with as many of your assumptions validated as possible by your own historical performance. It is the necessary financial component of a comprehensive business plan, and it serves the important function in your business of being a roadmap for getting where you want to go. Please refer to Table 30-3 to ensure it meets the IMPACT standard.

This can be compiled by simply preparing and linking several worksheets in a spreadsheet program, or you can also use one of many projection or modeling software programs. Be careful about getting too committed to one software program or another. Besides having to learn how to use the software, you may also find that it won't do what you need it to do after you've invested hours of time into it.

In addition to the three financial statement projections that need to be included in the model, you should have at least three supplemental worksheets to detail your assumptions. They include a main assumptions page, a marketing, sales, and cost of goods sold page, and a detailed payroll sheet.

Every 5-Year IMPACT Forecaster™ should have one page that contains all of the major assumptions for the model. If you are using Excel or another spreadsheet template to create the model, these assumptions should be linked throughout the model. This gives you the ability to make a change to any one of your assumptions and then see how that changes your profitability and cash flow outcomes throughout the plan.

When it comes to projecting your revenue and cost of goods sold, you need detail! It is not sufficient to say you're going to grow sales by 50%. What are the marketing activities that will drive that growth? How many leads will you need to generate the sales required to hit that growth rate? What is the cost of these required leads and other marketing activities? Which product or service lines will grow more than others? How does your gross margin differ on these lines as compared to slower-growth or even obsolete lines? Is there a difference in both the collections from customers and your payments to vendors and suppliers for costs of goods sold for those product lines? How will this impact cash flow? These are the questions, among many others, we look to this worksheet to answer.

How many people is it really going to take to accomplish what your financial model projects? What are the salary and wage costs to hire all of these people? Are your hiring practices in line with the sales per employee ratio according to our industry benchmark? Have you correctly factored in all payroll burden and benefit costs, including FICA, FUTA, SUTA, worker's compensation insurance, other state payroll taxes, health insurance, 401(k) match, etc.? Have you accurately forecasted all of the costs associated with adding these new employees, including recruiting, HR, and new office and computer equipment? All of these questions need to be factored into your plan so that you can demonstrate a realistic cost for growing your firm.

Of all three of these supplemental worksheets and all three major financial statements – the profit & loss, balance sheet, and statement of cash flow, you need to pay particular attention to the balance sheet. The balance sheet, not the P&L, is what drives the cash flow of the business. If the balance sheet is not correctly modeled, then the cash flow forecast is most likely inaccurate and worthless. Yet the balance sheet is the part of the model that is usually the most neglected and least understood.

In order to help get the balance sheet forecasting correct, I have identified three common mistakes that entrepreneurs, CEOs, business owners, and even business financial consultants make. They are: no balance sheet projections, failure to correlate operating activities on the P&L to changes in the operating assets and liabilities on the balance sheet, and disregard for the debt and equity transactions of the firm.

Yes, most often the biggest mistake is that the balance sheet is excluded altogether. The P&L shows profit, and many entrepreneurs think this is all they need to project. But profit never equals cash flow in the same period, so assuming the forecasted profit will be in your bank account, or the projected loss will deplete your bank account, is naïve. And, if you ever present your plan without a balance sheet to a bank or sophisticated investor, they will quickly lose confidence in you and your ability to do what you say you're going to do. Project what will happen to each balance sheet account as each one relates to the operations, investing, and financing activities of your company during the next five years.

TABLE 30-3

5-Year IMPACT Forecaster™		
I	Insightful	Includes P&L, Balance Sheet, Statement of Cash Flow, and many supporting worksheets; insights come in understanding key assumptions and in variance analysis
M	Meaningful	Month-by-month and annual summarized performance; focus on cash required to accomplish plan; milestone driven
P	Precise	Assumptions founded in historical data, benchmarks, market research; integrity in how all data ties and balances
A	Accessible	Physical--spreadsheet or software program; Intellectual--summarized information in charts and graphs
C	Comparative	Compare to prior periods; analyze variance from projection and improve assumptions, if necessary
T	Timely	Reviewed and updated at least quarterly

Another common mistake is not having the activities on the P&L of the firm accurately flow through the operating assets and liabilities on the balance sheet. The major operating assets include accounts receivable, inventory, pre-paid items, and more. The major operating liabilities include accounts payable, taxes payable, and other accrued expenses. When sales go up, accounts receivables should go up, and cash initially goes down. But does the model capture that? If sales go up, can you expect your inventory level to stay the same? Most likely it will need to increase over time. The increments of these changes are dependent upon the relationship between your days sales outstanding (DSO) and inventory turnover, which need to be included in your main assumptions worksheet previously discussed.

As sales increase, your accounts payable should increase because you are buying materials and using your suppliers and vendors more. The timing of when these costs are incurred and when they are actually paid influences your accounts payable and, ultimately, your cash flow. You need to define the relationship that payables have with your operating activities and implement this relationship in the balance sheet portion of the 5-year IMPACT Forecaster™.

There are several other operating assets and liabilities that dramatically impact cash flow that need to be tied to the growth and changes in the P&L. I'll avoid all of the details of each, but it's fair to say that without properly forecasting them, your projection will not be accurate and will lack the most critical information your model should include--cash flow.

Another area of the balance sheet that is often overlooked is the area that includes the loans, lines of credit, and equity transactions over the five-year period. Are you bringing in any more equity investments during the period you are modeling? What is your dividend policy for shareholders? Is some or all of the active shareholders' compensation coming through equity? All of these items can have a significant impact on cash flow, although none of them show up on the P&L.

In addition to equity transactions, the structure of all of the company's debts and obligations need to be correctly reflected on the balance sheet. An interest only line of credit will keep the same balance until more is withdrawn or some is paid back. Term loans need to show the correct amount of principal being reduced every month while the interest is reflected on the P&L. These types of transactions are complex, and accounting for them in the projection will help you improve the accuracy of the picture you are building for the future.

    This discussion of common mistakes is certainly not comprehensive (you'll notice I didn't address capital expenditures and depreciation at all), but should create a positive foundation to build the balance sheet portion of the model. The underlying point is that having a 5-Year IMPACT Forecaster™ is essential, but you will likely need some help to make sure you get the most value from it. And a side-benefit of having a CFO-level person help to design, build, and then track your performance against it is that you get their perspective on how other companies in the same and different industries build and then use their projections to create clarity. They will also help you bring your assumptions and projections into line with reality, always based on historical performance and benchmarks combined with your unique business.

31
IMPACT CFO SERVICES™

Jennifer helped Steve a great deal, but let's be honest. The longer Jennifer was helping Steve and the rest of the Bolty team implement the six essential scoreboards, the more valuable she became. Her understanding of how the business operated deepened each day she was there and, like any other employee Steve might hire, she had a learning curve associated with the inner workings of Bolty that she was quickly tackling.

Lots of consultants will do a month or two's worth of work and then leave, just as they were starting to overcome that learning curve. But Steve kept Jennifer around, and Jennifer wanted to be around--they both understood the value of a long-term relationship. She continued to work with Bolty as their outsourced or part-time CFO. Her responsibilities included overseeing all of the reporting functions of the firm and being part of the executive leadership team, specifically advising Steve as the CEO.

There are many benefits that come from having a CFO as part of your team. Because I operate in this industry, I will discuss all of these benefits in the context of stories of real scenarios and situations from my experiences as well as others I know and with whom I associate. You can use Table 31-1 as a guide to help your CFO meet the IMPACT standard.

Accounting/Finance Executive Leadership
When a CFO begins working for you, they immediately begin training and developing your company's staff to improve the accounting and reporting functions, with the initial focus on the six essential scoreboards. That evolves into a long term program to develop the staff to be more productive and add

more value to you, their employer, providing them a long-term career track within which they can grow professionally.

TABLE 31-1

IMPACT CFO Services™		
I	Insightful	Decade(s) of experience; perspective with great depth and breadth; serves your best interest
M	Meaningful	Focused on pivotal performance drivers of business; gives advice and direction on items that will being most value to business
P	Precise	Skilled in accounting and finance; Not perfectly precise all the time, but needs to be close
A	Accessible	Physical--in office as appropriate, runs and participates in meetings, responds to email, texts, phone calls within hours, not days; Intellectual--devotes significant strategic thought to your business
C	Comparative	Puts your company into context with industry, economy, and business community; draw upon successes and failures of others
T	Timely	Keeps commitments and is timely with all deliverables

The CFO should have a similar impact in the software and processes of each company for whom they work. They ensure your company maximizes its software and processes to help keep labor costs as low as possible without sacrificing the strategic benefits you should be receiving from your accounting and finance functions.

One part-time CFO started working with a company that had an accounting staff of one, and she was doing some data entry and some reconciliations without the benefit of much experience. Within a year she developed into a very strong Accounting Manager, with the potential to even grow into a Controller, with the CFO's leadership and guidance. The company has grown successfully and, with the CFO's help, she is beginning to hire and train additional staff to support the day-to-day transactions.

Sometimes executive leadership requires the CFO to teach the executive team how to interpret and analyze the six scoreboards. Another outsourced CFO began working with a very intelligent woman who had no financial or accounting experience prior to buying the business she now owns and operates. She was overwhelmed trying to understand the accounting and numbers of the business after she took over. It took some time, but with the help of her CFO she now understands concepts like gross margin, current ratio, and days sales outstanding, and she is making better business decisions because of it. Maybe that's part of the reason why she's doubled the business in the three short years she's owned it.

Relationship Manager with Outside Professionals
Entrepreneurs quickly realize they have to represent themselves to and manage their relationships with many different outside professionals, including bankers, CPAs, attorneys, insurance agents, payroll providers, consultants, and more. Each of these professionals speaks a certain language and is trying to accomplish certain objectives that may conflict with yours from time to time when it comes to doing business with them. Most entrepreneurs do not have the time nor do they want to become an expert in all of these fields to the extent required to effectively manage them. Entrepreneurs want to spend time growing their business, and that, quite honestly, is where they will have the most impact.

Handing these relationships off to others in your organization who are not qualified is not always the best idea. They may not have very much experience and may poorly represent your business and interests when working and negotiating with these professionals. A part-time CFO, however, can not only manage these relationships effectively, but he or she might even be able to get more from your current and future business dealings with them. Similar to the way Jennifer was able to speak in a language the bankers understood, she was able to get the short-term funds Bolty needed to get through the two-month cash crunch it faced.

A part-time CFO began working with a company that severely needed working capital. The company's banker was frustrated because the financial statements the company provided were inaccurate and the CEO was unable to understand how to portray his business to the bank. The banker actually recommended the CEO get some executive-level expertise.

The company's credibility was elevated significantly as soon as the CFO started and met with the banker. Once everything was cleaned up and presented correctly to the bank, with an eye for making sure the company's best foot was forward, the bank still tried to under-finance the company's need. The CEO was ready to accept the deal since his company was so cash-starved. But the CFO negotiated the terms and got the bank to issue a line of credit for more, giving the company all of the growth capital it required. Now the bank calls the CFO directly and doesn't even bother the CEO. The rest of our customers enjoy the same benefit.

A different part-time CFO helped a customer increase their line of credit by 150% because he knew how to communicate with and manage the banking relationship. And I know of countless additional examples, always with the results being improved because a CFO was involved in the process.

Another group that entrepreneurs struggle to understand and receive the most value from is CPAs. Similar to the direct relationship the CFO will have with your banker, the outsourced CFO is often the direct contact for the CPA. And there are two kinds of CPAs, tax and attestation. The tax CPA prepares your tax return(s) and helps with tax planning and other tax-related issues. The attestation CPA, which can be the same person as the tax CPA, performs consolidations, reviews, and audits of your firm.

An outsourced CFO received a referral from a tax CPA to one of his clients. In addition to all of the others ways the CFO helped this company, he began working directly with the CPA that referred him and has helped facilitate improved tax planning and a better result for the customer. The CPA appreciates what the CFO has been able to accomplish. He gets a cleaner, more accurate set of records from which to prepare the return, and his billable time with the client has increased because the CFO has included him in decisions for which he needed to have input as well as the tax planning meeting that is now held in his office in November of every year.

And the customer has benefitted, helping the company double its size in one year.

Some companies, although the number is small, are strong candidates to raise equity capital to start, grow, or accelerate their businesses. Your CFO should have helped other companies raise capital in the role of finance executive or CFO. Investors especially want to know that the financial and accounting side of the business is well-run with a CFO at the helm.

Trusted Advisor & Sounding Board

Owning and running a business is a difficult undertaking. You are immediately expected to make lots of decisions and become an expert in a lot of different areas. Many entrepreneurs do not have other executive-level people in their organizations because their businesses are not large enough to support the cost. As a result, these entrepreneurs have no one they can talk to that understands their business from the inside and can remain impartial to the nature of the conversation they might need to have to make an important decision.

Steve is a great example. Do you remember what happened when he started talking to Judy about the layoff? Judy freaked out and immediately became concerned, wanting to know if her name was on the list of those to be terminated. Her reaction wasn't abnormal or inappropriate, but Steve had to spend his energy trying to reassure her she was not going to be fired as opposed to being able to have a healthy, value-added discussion about the best course of action for the company. She could not effectively or strategically communicate any more on the subject from Steve's perspective. And Steve was frustrated, getting no advice or perspective on how he might approach this critical decision.

I have many examples from many CFOs who have filled this role of trusted advisor and sounding board for hundreds of businesses. In each scenario, the business owner or entrepreneur brings the CFO in for all major decisions as well as for advice on lots of other matters, including human resources, legal, marketing, sales, and more.

One part-time CFO met with a business owner that was paralyzed by fear. Not only did the CFO dispel the business owner's fear with clarity, he has become a trusted advisor on all topics related to the business. Thanks to his advice and perspective, the customer now has hope. As you can imagine, the CFO has become a critical member of this CEO's team.

Another CFO not only became the trusted advisor to the CEO of a company, but he fills that role with the board of directors as well. This company was embattled with equity and compensation issues, and the CFO successfully and amicably resolved all of the problems with and differences between all parties. He continues to be a sounding board on all of the company's major decisions.

This same CFO was originally hired by a family business to implement the six scoreboards. They found his perspective and advice so valuable, they wanted him to continue to be part of the business as the CFO. He continues to analyze and make improvements to their reporting and operational efficiencies, helping the business improve and grow.

Another outsourced CFO worked very closely with a partnership of two, one of whom was buying the other's interest in the venture. In addition to guiding them through this process, the CFO became a voice of reason to fix the mismanagement of marketing funds into extremely unproductive activities. With the marketing dollars redirected to the best initiatives, the business experienced unprecedented growth.

The reason the CFO becomes a sounding board and trusted advisor has one common thread--because the CFO knows the business inside-and-out and exists to serve its best interest. This trust is earned, and it is appreciated by every business using a part-time CFO.

Strategic Implementer

Talking about strategy is nice, but entrepreneurial companies need people working for them who know how to roll up their shirt sleeves and get things done. Figuring out the big picture of where the company wants to go is great, but that vision and strategy needs to be broken down into implementable tactics. A part-time CFO needs to help the company accomplish this.

As part of this role, the CFO is champion of the business model, helping the company stay on course with the most effective deployment of its model. The executive team of a respected company wanted to change the way some of the employees were paid. The CEO relied on the part-time CFO to analyze how it would impact the business model to see if it would work. Not only did the CFO help determine the new compensation program would not compromise the business model, he also helped create the roll-out of this new program and ensured all of the details were delegated and completed.

Entrance & Exit Developer

Getting into and out of businesses can be a complex process. The CFO can and should help you through any mergers, acquisitions, startups, joint ventures, IPOs, funding rounds, strategic alliances, and exits. All of our CFOs have consulted multiple businesses on the issues surrounding these transactions, including exhaustive due diligence and terms negotiations.

A growing company was offered a term sheet by a large, well-respected Private Equity group. The CFO was heavily involved in the due diligence, and took the lead on most of the process, seeing the deal through to the final signature.

Conclusion

Most entrepreneurs, owners, and CEOs of the start-up, emerging, and medium-sized companies that can benefit from a CFO don't even know what CFO stands for, let alone the difference one can make in their business. But, I can guarantee you that all of them have goals and objectives they want to accomplish with their ventures. It has been my experience, and the experience of a growing number of businesses around the world, that a part-time or outsourced CFO that delivers IMPACT CFO Services™ can improve performance and accelerate success.

Tools & Resources

32

ALLEGORICAL SYMBOLS

In addition to the four allegorical symbols to which I introduced you in the introduction, I wanted to share more background on the four already introduced as well as reveal several more for your consideration. You may want to think about which of these symbols exist, in reality, in your entrepreneurial venture.

Are you Steve, or can you relate to him? What is your family, or the most important thing in your life? Does a Judy Duke work for you? Do you have a peer like Jeff Hanks who you call for business and personal advice? I'll stop asking questions for now so you can read about the symbols.

Steve Loveland: Steve represents all of the entrepreneurs, business owners, and executives running small and medium-sized businesses. When the allegory begins, he's overwhelmed, depressed, frustrated, and tired. The burdens he carries are heavy, and he can't seem to find a way to lighten his load. All of this pressure almost makes it appear he is weak. However, as he begins to gain clarity, his confidence begins to return. He finds the passion he once had for business, and it makes all the difference. If you thought Steve was almost two different characters, that was, at least partially, intentional. Just see what clarity can unlock for you!

Jennifer Silverstone: Jennifer represents all of the finance executives that work exclusively with small and medium-sized businesses. She quickly earned Steve's trust because she was honest, bright, and added a great deal of value to his company. Her relationship with Steve and the entire team at

Bolty was strong, not like other outside or one-time consultants. Couldn't you see her comfortably attending Bolty's holiday party with her husband, Trent?

Loveland Family: All of the Lovelands, including Aubrye, Tyler, Zoe, Stacey, and Emma, represent the most important thing in an entrepreneur or business owner's life. Aubrye and Steve fought over money, mainly because they allowed their lifestyle to change as their income from Bolty increased. They had lost sight of their family as their greatest priority.

Aubrye Loveland: Aubrye played a critical role in waking Steve up to his neglect of that which was most important to him. It took Steve a while to realize what he was doing, even though Aubrye was more and more emphatically trying to get him to understand. She was a catalyst to help bring a necessary balance back into Steve's life. In many ways, the more he neglected everything else and became completely consumed with Bolty, the less effective he really was, not only at the business but everything else, too. As Steve disengaged from the business, his clarity actually increased and he became far more effective.

Bolty Solutions, Inc: To Steve, Bolty was almost like a child. It was part of his identity. He created it, grew it, and wanted so desperately for it to be successful. The emotional connection an entrepreneur has to his or her creation may not make sense to those who have never started or run a business, but it is real. And it sometimes needs to be put into check.

Tyler Loveland: Tyler was a tougher sell for Steve than most of Bolty's customers. Even when Steve was doing his absolute best as a father, Tyler could still make it difficult for his father to connect with him. When his son rejects him, it becomes quite tempting for Steve to hide-out in his home office and work on Bolty stuff. But he needs to resist the urge to give up, because eventually the investment of time and energy into whatever is most important will reap significant benefits and rewards.

Loveland Daughters: Zoe was the logical one, Stacey was the quiet one, and Emma was the one who lived in a fantasy world of princesses and ponies. Steve's three daughters represented the layers of and personalities associated with whatever is most important to you. If it is truly most important in your life, then its depth and breadth are probably far beyond one's abilities to completely comprehend, each layer peeled back revealing more to learn and understand. That's why you need to spend time with whatever you find most important, get to know it, and develop a relationship that is meaningful and life-changing.

Judy Duke: Judy represents all of the brave and loyal office managers, administrative managers, assistants, and others to whom the entrepreneur or business owner delegates the finance and accounting functions of the business. Judy lacked much formal training, most of her know-how coming in the form of on-the-job experiences, day-by-day. They are doing everything they can, but are not able, for a myriad of reasons, to implement the six scoreboards every business needs that meet the IMPACT criteria, even though their boss may expect them to.

Jeff Hanks: This is Steve's friend with whom he used to coach basketball. Jeff referred Jennifer to Steve and was a voice of reason and guidance. Jeff represents the network that people like Steve build, usually consisting of other business owners and entrepreneurs. With nowhere else to turn and few who really understand their problems, entrepreneurs often rely on their network of peers for help and guidance.

Terminated Employees: They represent the tough decisions business leaders must make to be effective. Accepting failure and cutting losses is often the most courageous act an entrepreneur can do.

Demoted Employee: Phil was over-promoted in the first place, justifying the return to his prior position. Over-promotion happens a lot in entrepreneurial companies, usually because it is assumed that if an employee is good at what she does, she'll be a good manager, too. This is often not the case, and few promoted managers will take a demotion and stay with the company, meaning the company ends up losing one of its best employees.

Employees Who Took Salary Reduction: This group represents all of the great people who work for small and medium-sized businesses. They usually have some form of relationship with the owner or CEO because the company is small enough that the leadership is still very accessible. These employees usually buy into the mission of the company and are willing to make sacrifices in their wages for the opportunity to help build something they want to be proud of.

Bankers: Rich and Zack represent all of the potential financing sources, both debt and equity, for a business. The sources speak a certain language, each having their own set of criteria and objectives for giving money to a business. They represent a complex world that most entrepreneurs struggle to maximize, primarily because they just don't know how to.

33
IMPACT INSIGHTS

For several years, I have felt compelled to convey the core concepts surrounding how entrepreneurs can obtain the clarity they need to effectively run their businesses and their lives. As I showed the allegory, in a much rougher state than you now see it, to some trusted friends and peers, they sensed that in addition to the main theme of the book the allegory was also full of general nuggets of entrepreneurial wisdom. When I went through the allegory, I found they were right, and the IMPACT Insights were born. I have identified forty-four of the most poignant and useful lessons throughout the text. Here is the complete list in the order they appeared in the allegory:

CHAPTER 3: PAYROLL
#1: Entrepreneurs carry great optimism toward their ventures, even when it seems like they should have no hope.

CHAPTER 4: MEETING
#2: Most people start businesses because it's their best option, not because they have a product or service that will take over the world.

#3: To grow beyond the point where the owner is involved in every detail of the business, every business must make a transition.

CHAPTER 6: CASH
#4: Many entrepreneurial companies can manage their cash flow more

efficiently than they currently are by maximizing what is referred to as the working capital cycle.

#5: Making working capital more efficient is only a one-time help to cash flow. A company that still has cash shortages after working capital is maximized almost always has bigger problems.

#6: Entrepreneurs usually like to make decisions quickly, but they can often benefit by waiting an extra couple of days for better information.

#7: Sometimes it takes the perspective of someone from outside the company to help an entrepreneur realize they need to make changes.

CHAPTER 7: TESTIMONIAL
#8: Entrepreneurs often struggle to separate business problems and family life, especially when their business is not doing well.

CHAPTER 9: GUT
#9: Being an entrepreneur is often a lonely endeavor, with few or no others that care about the business as much as the owner does.

#10: With a boot-strapping mentality, most start-up businesses require the founders to wear most, if not all, of the hats of responsibility.

#11: Being involved in every detail is cost effective for start-ups, but it teaches founders bad habits that can limit growth and opportunity.

#12: Not transitioning to the use of IMPACT quantitative data will eventually hinder an organization's ability to grow and keep the entrepreneur from building the most valuable business possible.

#13: When used correctly, quantitative data can improve performance, decision-making, acumen, and, most importantly, chances for success.

CHAPTER 10: IMPACT
#14: There is no problem in business that can't be quantified, affording the

clarity needed to overcome almost any challenge entrepreneurs face.

#15: Even if an entrepreneur is receiving some reports and quantitative information, they may not meet the IMPACT criteria, meaning the entrepreneur is not getting everything he should from the information.

#16: The IMPACT principles help every business ensure its quantitative data and reports are as effective and value-added as possible.

CHAPTER 11: INSIGHT

#17: Entrepreneurs often mask their business struggles well, a conditioned response for survival that can sometimes cause denial and blindness toward the problem.

CHAPTER 12: MEASUREMENTS

#18: Being a business leader means needing to make difficult decisions, and then following-through with them, regardless how unpleasant they may be.

#19: Most entrepreneurs take pride in providing jobs for employees and helping the economies in which they operate, and they do not like to let them down.

#20: Charts and graphs make it easy to process lots of information, quickly gaining the clarity required to improve the business.

#21: For a service business, gross margin, overhead, and backlog are very important numbers for making decisions with any type of financial ramifications.

CHAPTER 13: REDUCTION

#22: Break-Even, in dollars, is calculated by dividing the contribution margin (which is often the gross margin in service businesses) into the fixed costs. You can convert this to units by dividing the result by the average sales price per unit.

#23: Maximum profit per dollar of revenue will be attained when a company operates right at its capacity.

#24: After a layoff, the remaining employees need to see the firm has a solid plan for the future or they will leave, especially the top performers.

CHAPTER 14: FALL
#25: Building or re-establishing trust is not a one-time event. It is earned over time.

#26: Sacrifice is inherent with entrepreneurship, as business owners are usually the first to give something up for the betterment or even the survival of the company.

CHAPTER 16: AFTERMATH
#27: When all of the employees are interested in increasing sales, cutting costs, and the future of the company in general, silos between departments will be broken down, uniting the company.

#28: Even if they are only part-time, the CFO of entrepreneurial companies can significantly help the entrepreneur with all sorts of issues and problems.

CHAPTER 17: VALLEY
#29: Building an honest, open relationship with your lending institution usually proves to be best for all parties.

#30: Lending institutions usually secure collateral as a backup plan to recoup their money if an entrepreneur defaults on a loan. But they would always prefer the business be successful and pay them back in lieu of having to foreclose on or seize assets for which they probably can't get as much value as they need.

#31: A CFO knows how bankers think and what is important to them. Entrepreneurs who don't have a CFO are at a disadvantage when trying to work with bankers and lending institutions.

CHAPTER 18: CONFRONTATION

#32: Starting, nurturing, and growing a business is like raising a child, and entrepreneurs often allow the business to become an important part of their identity, just like proud parents do with their kids.

CHAPTER 19: SCOREBOARD

#33: At the core of the daily business scoreboard should be the key elements of the business model--how the company makes money.

CHAPTER 20: DAILY

#34: Employees and managers can benefit as much as entrepreneurs from the clarity the right quantitative data brings.

CHAPTER 21: METRICS

#35: Most entrepreneurs initially resist the change to less dependence on qualitative data. However, once they do it, they almost always wish they had done it sooner.

#36: The most effective weekly business metrics report should include data from every discipline, or department, of the company.

#37: The most successful entrepreneurs can fit all of the key business metrics they need to run their businesses onto one page.

#38: Many entrepreneurial companies use 50% or less of their employees' skills, experience, and overall abilities to help their businesses.

#39: The more employees feel the company is accomplishing a greater good, the more they will help the company succeed. And the more they help it succeed, the better the company becomes. They feed one another.

CHAPTER 22: DESSERT

#40: Every entrepreneur has something more important to him than his business. For Steve, it's his family. What is it for you?

CHAPTER 23: PROJECTIONS

#41: Fear and anxiety are negatively correlated to clarity. The more clarity an entrepreneur has, the less fear and anxiety he will feel.

#42: Planning for the future and then tracking performance against that plan will help entrepreneurs gain competitive advantages.

#43: Financial Modeling is not pretending to have a crystal ball for the future. It is about understanding the impact certain decisions will have on the future as well as helping the company chart the best course possible in its strategic and tactical initiatives.

#44: The most valuable thing a part-time CFO gains while helping to establish the six scoreboards is knowledge about how the business works and what makes it successful. This is wasted if the entrepreneur does not continue to have that CFO be part of his executive team on an ongoing basis.

34
GLOSSARY

To ensure anyone can pick up this book and understand what it is trying to communicate, I have assembled this glossary. But it is not just a normal glossary of accounting and finance of terms. It also includes a brief discussion on each of the major symbols of the allegory, not in alphabetical order.

Accrual-Basis Accounting: This is a step up from cash-basis accounting in terms of coming closer to reporting true performance on a month-by-month basis. It recognizes revenues when they are earned regardless of when they are actually received. It recognizes expenses when they are incurred, not when they are paid. In addition, it works to match the earned revenues with the costs incurred to earn that revenue, and it correctly recognized period costs in the correct periods, not when they are paid. This type of accounting relies more heavily on the balance sheet than cash-basis accounting.

Backlog: This represents the total amount of work a company has contracted or scheduled to complete. It is derived by taking the total amount of work not yet completed, adding new work awarded, and subtracting work completed. It is also a "going-out-of-business" test to see how much longer the company will survive if it brings on no new work. Here is the formula:

Backlog=Total Work Started - Work Completed + Work Not Started

Balance Sheet: This is a snapshot of the aggregation of all of a company's activities through a specified point in time. It shows balances in several types of accounts, which are broken up into three main categories: assets, liabilities, and equity. It should be the main focus of generating precise monthly financial statements, with an emphasis on reconciling every balance sheet account every month.

Break-Even: This can be stated in dollars or units, and it represents the amount of sales volume a company needs to generate in order to cover all of its expenses, with a final net income of zero for the period. Please note that cash flow break-even differs from this number, primarily because it does not include principal payments on debt and distributions and dividends taken by partners, members, or shareholders.

Cash-Basis Accounting: This method of accounting recognizes revenue when it is received, not when it is earned, and expenses when they are paid, not when they are incurred. Most small businesses file their tax returns on this basis, meaning they need to keep cash-basis books for compliance purposes. Cash-basis reporting, however, never gives a clear picture of actual performance, meaning most companies get more strategic value from using accrual-based accounting methods for their internal reporting purposes.

CFO: Stands for Chief Financial Officer, the CFO is the executive that oversees the accounting and finance functions of the firm and is a critical member of the company's leadership team, helping to set strategic initiatives and then oversee the tactical and strategic implementation of those initiatives. Refer to Chapter 29 for more information about what a CFO does and how it should benefit the company.

Current Assets: A sub-section of the asset section on the balance sheet, these accounts are either cash or will be converted to cash in the next 12 months or less. These accounts include cash and cash equivalents, accounts receivable, inventory, work-in-progress (WIP), pre-paid assets, inter-company loans, and more.

Current Liabilities: A sub-section of the liabilities section on the balance sheet, these accounts must be paid within 12 months or less. These accounts include accounts payable, credit cards, payroll accruals, payroll tax liabilities,

---

deferred revenue, short-term portion of long-term debt, inter-company loans, and more.

Current Ratio: This is a metric used to measure the overall liquidity of your company. It is determined by taking your current assets divided by your current liabilities. It determines how many times your cash and other current assets will cover your current liabilities. Banks often require a ratio of 1.25 or greater in order for them to loan you money.

Days Sales Outstanding (DSO): This is a financial metric that measures, on average, how long it takes for you to receive payment after you invoice a customer. It is calculated by taking the average accounts receivable balance, dividing by the total sales, and then multiplying that result by the total number of days in the period being measured.

Debt: Also known as the liability section on the balance sheet, this is one of the two ways to fund the operations of a business. It implies borrowing money from an outside source for a period of time, and then repaying that amount at a future date, with or without interest as agreed upon by the parties involved.

Depreciation: This is a non-cash expense that represents the cost of owning a fixed asset in the period being measured. There are several ways to account for depreciation, but the straight-line method is usually the best for gaining strategic insights and fairly accounting for the costs of fixed asset ownership. Your business may benefit from more accelerated treatment of depreciation for tax.

Discounted Cash Flow (DCF): This is a method, based on the strength of a company's ability to generate future cash flows, of valuing a business. The further into the future the cash flow will be generated the less that cash is worth in today's dollars based on the time-value of money and the risk premium associated with the business being valued.

EBITDA: This is an acronym for Earnings Before Interest, Taxes, Depreciation, and Amortization. As mentioned in this book, it is also known as the lazy man's short cut to cash flow. It is frequently used in the valuation of business, assigning a multiple to the prior year's EBITDA results to determine the value of the future cash flows of the business.

Entrepreneur: I own a book that takes the first fifty pages trying to determine and then explain what an entrepreneur is. Here's what I think. An entrepreneur is anyone who comes up with an idea to solve a problem in the world and then creates a commercially-viable business model around solving that problem for its customers. Please note that there are many entrepreneurs within large corporations who fit this broad description as well as millions around the world founding completely new companies each year. This can include single-person businesses, known as solo-preneurs, mom and pop lifestyle businesses, and venture entrepreneurs, like the founders of Google, who grow their companies into global powerhouses.

Equity: Also known as net worth, it is the difference between the book value of the assets and the liabilities/debt of the company. It appears on the bottom of the balance sheet and is one of two means whereby a business is financed.

ERP: This stands for Enterprise Resource Planning system, which is the type of accounting and business management software that businesses merge into when they outgrow the standard, off the shelf accounting software packages. These systems, which are made by a number of different companies, are designed to integrate all of the business functions, including marketing, sales, operations, human resources, accounting, finance, and more into one holistic system comprising of enterprise-wide management and planning.

Fixed Assets: Also known as Property, Plant, and Equipment (PP&E), Fixed Assets are assets on the balance sheet that will likely not be directly converted into cash in twelve months or less. The fixed assets are critical in helping the firm generate cash flow through operations, but they are not primarily converted directly to cash as part of the operations of the firm. Examples include vehicles, computers, heavy equipment, permanent improvements made to a building, and more.

Gross Margin: This measures gross profit as a percentage of sales and is one of the core ratios that every entrepreneur needs to understand intimately. Gross profit is the remaining contribution toward all of the overhead expenses in a firm after costs directly related to sales, also known as cost of sales or costs of goods sold, are subtracted from net sales.

IMPACT: The acronym representing the six criteria to which the six essential scoreboards need to adhere, it stands for **I**nsightful, **M**eaningful, **P**recise, **A**ccessible, **C**omparative, and **T**imely.

Maximum Capacity: The most amount of work an organization can do or units it can produce without having to add to the fixed cost structure of the firm. This is almost always the most profitable point for a company.

Personal Guarantee: A requirement of almost all bank loans, it obligates the entrepreneur to become responsible for all debts for which the business defaults.

Profit and Loss Statement (P&L): Always set to a specific period of time, it represents the revenues and expenses of the firm. It is the easiest to understand of the three main financial statements (P&L, Balance Sheet, and Statement of Cash Flows), which is why it is the most popular among and most referenced by entrepreneurs.

Tax CPA: The individual or firm licensed as a Certified Public Accountant that prepares the company's annual tax return and gives the company advice on all tax related matters. As a best practice, entrepreneurs should meet with their tax CPA at least once before the tax year is over to plan for and implement strategies surrounding taxes.

Working Capital: General finance defines this as current assets minus current liabilities, and it inherently illuminates the liquidity of a company.

Working Capital Cycle: Also referred to as the cash conversion cycle, this measures the amount of time it takes from when the company pays for costs to when the company receives payment from customers related to incurring those costs. Most businesses have a positive working capital cycle, meaning they pay money out to employees, suppliers, and vendors before they ever receive revenue from a customer. Some businesses, like mail order companies that wait to produce the products purchased until after they are paid, can carry a negative working capital cycle.

ACKNOWLEDGEMENTS

Not unlike a tall tree that begins as a very small seed, the idea for this book was, at one time, a very small seed. It has been nurtured and tended to by many who have so positively influenced my life. I will name a few, but please know there are so many more.

I thank all of the entrepreneurs who are currently my customers. They are an inspiration and worthy of emulation. Their ongoing concerns continue to be my most passionate interest along with those of my partners and colleagues at CFOwise®. They all have been supportive and a wealth of knowledge and insight.

My editor, Jennifer Leigh-Mustoe, deserves nothing short of a medal for her patience and expertise. Jenevieve Hubbard of Blackbird Creative did a great job on the book cover, and Kim Waldron was so valuable with the interior book design and preparing the book to publish in print as well as so many e-book formats.

My father is my example, and I am forever blessed that he shattered the cycle. He and my mother, the perfect team, raised me to find the good and positive in everything.

My wife has been through countless brainstorming and editing sessions, and has been a voice of reason and support throughout my professional life. Her compassion and depth have no limits. Thanks to her, our children will turn out far better than me. I'm already trying to catch up to her and them, and they make everything in my life worthwhile.

ABOUT THE AUTHOR

K en Kaufman currently serves as the CFO for ten entrepreneurial ventures. He founded CFOwise®, which has received the prestigious Top 25 Under Five award for three consecutive years. In 2010 he was included in the Utah Business Top Forty Under 40 and vSpring's v|100, a peer-selected group of the top 100 venture entrepreneurs.

Ken earned a B.S. in business from BYU and an MBA from the University of Georgia in finance and entrepreneurship where he was the most outstanding MBA student of his class. He has committed his career to helping the rising generation of entrepreneurs realize their full potential, part of which comes through successfully transitioning to the six essential scoreboards every business needs. He speaks and writes frequently and, in between a weekly date-night with his wife, coaching one or more of his six kids' sports teams, and other church and volunteer activities, he finds enough time to teach Entrepreneurial Finance at Utah Valley University.

$350+ VALUE

To help you begin the *Impact Your Business* journey, I would like to give you access to the members only section of the CFO*wise*® website for only the cost you incurred to obtain this book. It is rare that you will be able to receive more than a ten times return immediately on any investment you make, but that's exactly what this offer represents. With access to the website, you will be able to benefit from the following tools and resources:

- Industry Data & Analysis Report, valued at $200.00
- Discount on IMPACT Products, valued at $150.00
- Sample IMPACT Indicators™ Reports
- Sample IMPACT Forecaster™ Reports
- Bi-monthly newsletter to help you *Impact Your Business*
- E-books on topics related to *Impact Your Business*
- Additional tools and resources

To take advantage of this exclusive offer, please visit the website below, click on the link to the *Impact Your Business* book, and enter the following code when prompted:

Website: CFO*wise*.com
Password: imp@cturb1z

ABOUT CFO*wise*®

Shortly after the birth of our first child, my wife and I welcomed two black lab puppies to our first home which we purchased less than six months earlier. With no fence to enclose our backyard, the young puppies were still easy to mange and keep track of when they were outside. But the bigger they grew, the more I realized we needed a fence.

Even though I didn't know the first thing about building a fence, I figured doing the work myself would be the most economical way to get the job done. So in the middle of a very cold winter in Utah and with the help of a brother-in-law who was a pretty good 'do-it-yourselfer', we constructed a simple wood fence around the house.

I quickly became overwhelmed with the project, and I'm a little embarrassed to admit that the fence did not turn out very well. In fact, when we occasional drive past that home we sold about a decade ago, I cringe when I see slats that have broken off and the crooked gate I tried, but failed so miserably, to hang level.

I realize that the contents of this book may feel overwhelming, especially if you are new to some of the concepts and principles being taught. Building that fence taught me that getting help is usually an effective way to get things done. I ended up spending about the same amount of money it would have cost to have a professional do the entire job, and I could have used all that time and mental bandwidth expended on the fence project on something far more productive and valuable.

If you want to implement all of the principles in this book on your own, I wrote this book for you. I hope it helps you tackle each of the principles, concepts, and tactics it teaches. But if you would like a little guidance along the way, or if you would like to hire a professional to come in and take care of it all for you, I founded CFOwise® to be a resource for you.

For the last several years the CFOwise® team has had the opportunity to work with, serve, and represent some of the finest entrepreneurs of the 21st century. During this time we have found common challenges and issues that every entrepreneur faces. In response, we have designed, refined, and delivered the following suite of products that can help entrepreneurs and business owners obtain the clarity they need to maximize their cash and achieve their desired objectives. Each of these products, as listed below, adheres to the six IMPACT criteria.

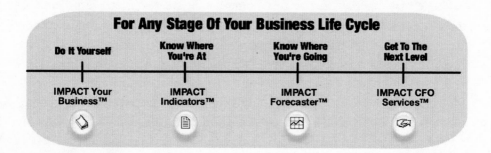

Regardless of where your business is in its life cycle, you can benefit from the clarity that the IMPACT products provide. To learn more about these products and the costs associated with each, please visit www.CFOwise.com.